CREATING CHARACTERS KIDS WILL LOVE

Here's a no-nonsense, straightforward, take-no-prisoners book on creating interesting and believable characters when writing for children. It has everything the beginning writer needs to know. I shall be recommending it to my own writing students.

—Jane Yolen, author of *Owl Moon*,
The Devil's Arithmetic, Touch Magic and two hundred other books

Buy a new highlighter; you'll need it. Creating Characters Kids Will Love *is much more than a book on how to craft characters—it moves on to character growth, series characters, plot development, point of view and more. This is not a writing book for your shelf. You'll want it on your desk to refer to every day.*

—Audrey B. Baird, editor of
Once Upon A Time, a national magazine for children's writers
and illustrators, and author of *Storm Coming!*

"Excellent advice for any writer!"

—Anastasia Suen, author of
Window Music, a *Time Magazine* Best Children's Book of the Year

Elaine Marie Alphin is one of those rare combinations—a fine writer who is also an excellent teacher. She has the ability to analyze the writing process and guide others through its complexities. Creating Characters Kids Will Love *is clear, thorough, and inspiring.*

—Sandy Asher, author of
Stella's Dancing Days and editor of *With All My Heart, With All My Mind:
Thirteen Stories About Growing Up Jewish*

Following just a few of the many "Try It Yourself!" exercises will help writers get to know their characters inside and out. I started recalling events from my own school days I'm not so sure I wanted to remember— the pain of youth! As a nonfiction writer, I found the tips on research and interviewing especially helpful.

—Brandon Marie Miller, author of
Buffalo Gals

Elaine's book is a much-needed one, specifically for those of us who write for children. Creating believable kids is more complex than many writers think. Seldom do writers give nearly enough thought to motivation and believability, yet Elaine tackled that very thing in Chapter 1!

—Kristi Holl, author of
Stage Fright and Web editor for The Institute of Children's Literature
(www.institutechildrenslit.com)

Elaine Alphin has written in Creating Characters Kids Will Love *an incredibly thorough and insightful book on creating characters for the children's writer. I found example after example illuminating and inspiring, and the exercises at the end of each chapter create a wealth of additional resources that students can use to put into action what they have read. I applaud Elaine Alphin for providing a wonderful resource on an overlooked area for children's writers. Don't be without it!*

Barbara Seuling, author of
How to Write a Children's Book and Get It Published

Creating Characters Kids Will Love

Elaine Marie Alphin
author of *Counterfeit Son*

WRITER'S DIGEST BOOKS

Cincinnati, Ohio
www. writersdigest.com

Creating Characters Kids Will Love. Copyright © 2000 by Elaine Marie Alphin. Manufactured in the United States of America. All rights reserved. No part of this book may be reproduced in any form or by any electronic or mechanical means including information storage and retrieval systems without permission in writing from the publisher, except by a reviewer, who may quote brief passages in a review. Published by Writer's Digest Books, an imprint of F&W Publications, Inc., 1507 Dana Avenue, Cincinnati, Ohio 45207. (800) 289-0963. First edition.

Visit our Web site at www.writersdigest.com for information on more resources for writers.

To receive a free weekly E-mail newsletter delivering tips and updates about writing and about Writer's Digest products, send an E-mail with "Subscribe Newsletter" in the body of the message to newsletter-request@writersdigest.com, or register directly at our Web site at www.writersdigest.com.

04 03 02 01 00   5 4 3 2 1

Library of Congress Cataloging-in-Publication Data

Alphin, Elaine Marie
  Creating characters kids will love / by Elaine Marie Alphin.—1st ed.
    p. cm.
  Includes index.
  ISBN 0-89879-985-6 (pbk.: alk. paper)
    1. Children's literature—Authorship. 2. Characters and characteristics in literature. I. Title: Colorful characters. II. Title.

  PN147.5 .A43 2000
  808.06′83—dc21

00-042251
CIP

Edited by Michelle Howry
Designed by Matthew Gaynor
Cover designed by Lisa Buchanan
Cover illustration by Guy Porfirio
Production coordinated by Kristen Heller

FOR J. DENNIS HUSTON,
who taught me so much about writing—
most of all, the importance of
pushing myself to write better than I believed I could.

ACKNOWLEDGMENTS

I wrote this book under challenging circumstances while I lived in a series of hotels in Northern Virginia, helping my mother-in-law recover from a devastating automobile wreck. I could not have completed this project without the help of a number of people, and I would like to take this opportunity to thank them.

First and foremost, I would like to thank the members of my writers' group in Bloomington, Indiana: Elsa Marston, Pam Service, Marilyn Anderson, Pat McAlister, Keiko Kasza, and Marcia Kruchten. Even though I was 700 miles away from them, these writers kept in touch, offered encouragement and support, read my drafts, and added their insights and ideas to mine.

I would also like to thank Jean Gralley, friend and fellow writer, who lived nearby in Virginia and was generous with her time, her food, her support, and her feedback on portions of this manuscript.

I would like to thank the virtual fellowship of writers in the Pod and in WRT4KDZ. I'm privileged to be a part of these online writers' groups, and I thank the members who answered questions, made thought-provoking comments, and offered encouragement on this project.

I would like to thank my writing students at the Institute of Children's Literature, whose successes and setbacks over the years have shown me so much about creating believable characters. I would like to thank Pamela Kelly for getting me started as a teacher. I would also like to thank Susan Tierney, who convinced me to progress from teaching writing to writing about writing in Children's Writer. I've learned a great deal from my readers. And I would like to thank the many SCBWI Regional Advisors who have invited me to speak to their members. I've always learned as much as I've taught during these conferences.

I would like to thank all the writers whose books I've cited here. Thank you for creating such compelling and endearing characters that they made their home in my heart, and made me want to share them with so many readers.

I would like to thank the editors at Writer's Digest Books: Michelle Howry who offered guidance and enthusiasm for the project, and made it easy for us to work together despite my uncertain schedule as a caregiver; Jack Heffron who originally contacted me and invited me to write this book, and who has made me feel so welcome in the Writer's Digest family of authors; and Alice Pope who invited me to speak to her Cincinnati SCBWI group, and who casually asked if I had any ideas for a book I'd like to write for Writer's Digest about writing for kids.

Finally, I would like to thank my husband, Arthur B. Alphin. Despite the long weeks apart, broken only by too brief visits, he remained encouraging, supportive of my work, and unfailingly helpful in more mundane matters, such as setting up my iMac and my printer in various hotel rooms, and moving boxes of books and files from my office at home to my office-on-the-go in Virginia. As always, his confidence in me enables me to accomplish far more than I ever think possible.

ABOUT THE AUTHOR

Elaine Marie Alphin's first novel, *The Ghost Cadet*, was published by Henry Holt and was nominated for awards in thirteen states, winning the Virginia Best Book Award. Her second Holt novel, *The Proving Ground*, was an ALA Recommended Book for Reluctant Young Adult Readers. *A Bear for Miguel*, a HarperCollins I Can Read Book, was a Consortium of Latin American Studies Programs Commended Title and has appeared on two state award lists. Her nonfiction books include *Vacuum Cleaners*, *Toasters*, *Irons*, and *Telephones* in Carolrhoda's "Household History" series. Harcourt Brace has just released her latest novel, *Counterfeit Son*.

Alphin is the "Commentary" columnist for *Children's Writer*. More than 200 of her stories, articles, puzzles, and activities for kids have appeared in national magazines including *Cricket*, *Spider*, *Ladybug*, *Highlights*, *Faces*, *Child Life*, *Children's Digest*, *Guideposts for Kids*, *Hopscotch*, *Boys' Quest*, *Disney Adventures*, and others. As a Society of Children's Book Writers and Illustrators member, she was awarded the SCBWI Magazine Merit Award for Fiction for "A Song in the Dark" (*Young & Alive*) and for Nonfiction for "Cornflower's Test" (*Cricket*), and a Works-in-Progress Grant for *The Ghost Cadet*.

Alphin's stories appear in such anthologies as *But That's Another Story* (Walker), *Rainy Day / Sunny Day / Any Day Activities* (Concordia), and *Success Stories* (ICL). Forthcoming books include *Dinosaur Hunter* for Harper-Collins, *Besieged by a Ghost* for Henry Holt, and *Around the World in 1500* and *Around the World in 1800* for Marshall Cavendish. Elaine Marie Alphin lives in Madison, Indiana, with her husband, Art, surrounded by squirrels, chipmunks, geese, and the past and future characters of her imagination.

CONTENTS

Hey kids look at this!

INTRODUCTION

As a child, I read to make new friends who shared my hopes, my fears, my insecurities and my fascinations. I read to experience adventures far beyond my ordinary life and to imagine that I, too, could rise to the heights of bravery, leadership, cleverness and steadfastness demonstrated by the boys and girls in the pages of my favorite books and stories.

As I started to write this book, however, I couldn't help but wonder if today's kids get caught up in their reading in the same way. Twenty-first-century kids lead fast-paced lives. They click the remote on the TV if the story isn't moving fast enough; they jump and shoot in rapid-fire video games; they're used to the hyper-fast hyperlinks on the Internet. Do they even take time to read? My answer came from the excited faces of children in the schools where I spoke and from the letters youngsters wrote me—and it was a resounding *yes*.

What makes a kid slow down and curl up with a book? A good story is important, but it's not the only thing that matters, or kids would click a mental remote with books when the story pace slows down, as fast as they click the channel remote on TV. What is it that engages their hearts? A twelve-year-old boy from Pennsylvania wrote to me:

1

> I really like your book, *The Ghost Cadet*. I have read it three times and each time I found something new and interesting. Benjy Stark is a lot like me. In many ways we have the same feelings. In some ways, I feel like my own parents have deserted me like everyone else. I really like your book and will continue reading it and enjoying it.

Was it really my book that boy liked so much? No—he liked Benjy Stark. Benjy wasn't just a paper character to him. The kid identified with Benjy.

Kids read because a magical closeness springs up between them and the characters in books and stories—the same magical closeness I felt as a child. They read because a writer has brought a character to life on the page for them. This writer has created a person readers want to know better—someone they identify with, or someone they would like to have for a friend perhaps, someone who's like the kids they know in school, maybe even like someone they know and hate.

An eleven-year-old boy from Illinois wrote to me:

> I like Miss Leota. I liked how she had a firm personality. She was nice, in a strict way. I also liked Benjy because he had the ability to stay occupied on bad-weather days. That may seem weird, but I can hardly ever, other than reading, stay occupied on a rainy day. Benjy was also very smart. I admire that, too!
>
> I think Hugh was the best character. He always talks about himself as a failure, but in reality I would be really freaked about going to war for my country!
>
> Then there was Fran. I did not like Fran because she always screamed and yelled to get her way. She was stubborn, like my brother.

This reader measures himself to Benjy and Hugh, and compares Benjy's sister to his own brother. He has made these characters his own. Kids often tell me what they wish my characters had done, and they beg me to write sequels in which they get a chance to do this. My characters have come to life for these readers, and the kids want to hold on to them. This book will show you how to create characters for your stories and books that readers will make their own and long to see more of. And you won't just read my advice about how to do it—you'll start doing it yourself.

Writers write—and writers read. I have taken this counsel to heart in writing this book, and I hope you'll take it to heart in reading it.

Throughout you'll find recommendations for you to "Read the Pros." I've cited examples of writers who accomplish what I have endeavored to explain. I hope you'll raid your library shelves for these books and enjoy meeting the characters in their pages.

Throughout you'll also find invitations to "Try it Yourself." You certainly don't have to do all of these writing exercises, but remember that writers write. The more you practice the techniques you see in this book, the greater the ease with which you'll populate your stories and books with believable characters. Hopefully you'll enjoy these opportunities to jump in and write. Just stretch your imagination and flex your growing skills at character craft, and you'll be on your way to developing strong, compelling characters that young readers will be eager to meet.

PART I
Characters in Search of a Plot

BELIEVABLE KIDS ON THE PAGE

Finding Story Characters

Story characters can come to life for the child who reads about them.

Remember wanting to go on escapades with Pippi Longstockings? Longing to escape down the river with Huck Finn? Clutching your notebook and yearning to find out everything about the people you saw, like Harriet the Spy? These characters became your friends. And you want your characters to befriend the children who read your book or story.

But where do these characters come from? If you sit down and start to write, who will you write about?

Potential story characters are all around you. You see them walking to school; you see them shopping in the mall; you see them biking or skating down your street. If you close your eyes, you see them in your memory—the child you once were, the friends you remember, the children you've raised or the children you've known. Believable characters are born from real people and revealed to readers through your writer's craft.

When you do this well, your reader will identify with your main character, and she will feel that character's fear and elation as she struggles to succeed in the book. As the characters in your story grow and change, the reader will share that growth. To make this magic happen, you need to believe in the characters whose story you're writing. You need to know them intimately. And you need to show them to your reader.

Characters do things

The first step in bringing a character to life is deciding what the character will do in your story. Characters are rarely passive; they take action. And the reader, as well as the other characters in the story, forms an impression of this character based on his actions. When you meet a new kid for the first time, you pay attention to what the newcomer does. If the new boy runs screaming to the teacher when he gets tripped in the school yard, you label him a crybaby. If the new girl shows off her rows of pierced earrings, her spiked hair and her ticket stubs and backstage passes from the hottest rock star (who only played New York and Los Angeles), you know she's a braggart, and you wonder if she's really telling the truth. These actions reveal the personality behind them.

When you write a story, you probably have an idea of how the plot will develop, but you're still getting to know your characters. Suppose you decide to write about a boy sneaking out of a locked house to meet a friend—he'll have to climb out of the window and down the roof. At this stage, you as the writer are moving your character around like a playing piece on the vast gameboard of your plot. You're directing the action. If you leave it at that, however, you'll end up with a cardboard character who's about as believable as a rook in a chess game. To make that boy believable, you need to look inside of him and make him want to take those actions.

After you direct the larger action of the story, plan what specific actions your character will take in order to develop the plot. Now transform your role from director to actor. Ask yourself how your character will perform these actions—with the skill of a third grader tying his shoes, or with the hesitancy of a kindergartner writing his name on the blackboard? If your main character has to climb down a roof, how will he do it? First think about the series of actions needed to climb down a roof, from opening the window to climbing through and across the roof's surface. As you sit at your keyboard, move your arms and legs, stretching them as you imagine you might if you were climbing. Make note of these actions.

Why is your character doing this?

To show your character's actions in the context of his personality, you'll have to know some background about him. Ask yourself questions in order to find out what experience he's had. Has he climbed down a roof before, or is this the first time? Is he scared of heights, or does he revel in them? Then think about his motivation—why is he climbing down this roof? Why is it so important to him to meet that friend? Is he climbing down the roof because he likes the idea of taking a risk? Does he want to see what it will feel like? What's at stake—what will happen if he doesn't succeed? Is his reason compelling? If not, will he decide partway through that he's had enough and he's turning back?

There are many ways you could develop this scene to show the reader something about a character. In *The Ghost Cadet*, I wrote a scene about Benjy, my twelve-year-old main character, like this:

His sneakers were braced against the roof's shingles. Slowly, Benjy took one hand off the sill and gripped a lower shingle instead. Then he took a deep breath, told himself very firmly not to be afraid, and let go of the sill with his other hand.

There was a bad moment when his free hand couldn't seem to find a shingle, but Benjy made himself stay calm, and finally his damp palm slid down one row of shingles and he hooked his fingers over the next one and held tight. After that, inching his way down row by row didn't seem so terrible.

His sneaker scraped a loose shingle once, and he was afraid everyone had heard. For a second he clung to the roof, waiting for the lights to flash on, but the unexpected noise must have sounded loud only in his own ears, because the house remained dark and silent.

One foot finally brushed the gutter, and Benjy knew he had to look down. He steadied his grip and turned his head, and breathed a sigh of relief. He was positioned directly over the concrete bench. Carefully he lowered himself until he was hanging from the edge of the roof by both hands. His feet dangled just above the bench.

Why couldn't he have been a few inches taller? Benjy cursed his height silently. Even just a couple of inches would have meant his toes might have been able to feel the bench beneath him. But wishing wouldn't make him grow. Benjy looked down one last time and asked himself whether this was really necessary. Flexing his arms, knees, and body, he ordered himself to relax, and took a deep breath, and let go.

You can tell that Benjy is afraid from his slow progress, and that he probably hasn't done this before from his awkward movements. You can see his frustration about being short. You can see the way he talks himself into doing what he doesn't want to do. Determining specific actions and attitudes like this helps you know how your character will be able to do something else in the story. For instance, the next time he has to climb something, he'll probably do it more quickly and use more confident movements. Perhaps his inner voice won't need to talk him into doing something dangerous, but will cheer him on for doing it well. You'll build on the actions your characters take in order to develop these characters for the reader and to show how they grow as people in the course of your story.

Read the Pros

1. Read the opening chapters of Chaim Potok's *My Name Is Asher Lev*. Asher is a small child who will grow up to be a great artist. See how he describes the people around him, particularly his parents, solely in terms of their actions. Potok doesn't tell the reader the conclusions Asher will later draw from these observations; he just shows the actions and lets the reader bring Asher's parents into focus as Asher does.

2. Read chapter 2 in *Homecoming* by Cynthia Voigt. See how much Voigt shows the reader about Dicey's brothers and sister though their actions.

TRY IT YOURSELF: CHARACTERS DO THINGS

1. Write your own scene of a character climbing down a roof. Make the character a ten-year-old boy doing it on a dare from his friends. Then try it again, making it a fourteen-year-old girl climbing down her roof while her room is on fire. Choose another reason why a youngster of any age might climb down that roof, then let him or her make the climb.

2. Describe a five- or six-year-old taking a specific action, such as:
   * finger painting
   * putting together a puzzle
   * swinging in a playground
   * playing tag
   * jumping rope
   * bouncing a ball
   * playing with a puppy

3. Describe an adolescent taking a different specific action, such as:
   * turning on a computer and working at it
   * playing beach volleyball
   * getting a backpack ready for school
   * building a bird feeder
   * playing keep-away

Characters think

In the example from *The Ghost Cadet*, Benjy doesn't only act—he also thinks about his actions. He tries to talk himself into courage, and he curses his lack of those last few inches that would make it easier for him to drop down from the roof. Action in a vacuum allows the reader to see the character from the outside. That's fine for secondary characters who are seen through your main character's perspective. But this isn't quite enough to bring your main character to life. The reader identifies with your protagonist and wants to share that character's thoughts. To open your character's mind to the reader, you have to get inside it and express those thoughts.

A character may have fundamental religious or philosophical beliefs in the beginning of the story that will be challenged before the end. For example, middle-grade Jennifer, whose parents have never attended church, may believe she's an atheist. When she makes a friend who goes to church every Sunday, attends Youth Group and prays in the cafeteria before lunch, Jennifer may start to wonder if there really is a God. Or Ryan, a tough adolescent who believes in machismo and likes to wrestle, could discover the other best wrestler in school is gay. Ryan might start out despising gays and slowly change his mind and accept the other boy as a friend. Or these kids may not change. But they will start out with strong thoughts about the matter, thoughts they'll question in the course of your story.

Your characters don't necessarily say what they think. Jennifer's friend may talk about her religious beliefs, but she may have private doubts she doesn't express. She may wonder whether or not God hears her when she prays. She may envy her new friend's freedom on Sunday morning to sleep late. Or her faith may run deeper than she'll admit to her parents or her friend—she may be considering joining a cult. All your characters' thoughts, whether hidden or spoken, will contribute to the tension and drama of your story.

What do they think about each other?

In addition to fundamental beliefs, your characters have opinions about the people around them. A character may like certain classmates based on the sort of clothes or glasses they wear, the sports they play, their hobbies or their shared interests. A youngster has strong opinions about his teachers based on how much homework each teacher assigns, how hard the tests are, how interesting the teacher makes the class or how funny the teacher's jokes are.

Closer to home, a character sees her parents in certain ways. She may judge each of them by whether or not the family does things together, what

TRY IT YOURSELF: CHARACTERS THINK

1. Create a set of ethics for a potential character in a story. How does he determine right and wrong? What does he believe about God? What general expectations does he hold about people (basically nice or basically evil)?

2. Who's your character's best friend? What does he think about this best friend? Do they agree about everything? Do they agree to disagree about some things? Why does your character think they became best friends? Why does his best friend think they are best friends?

3. What does your character think about these teachers?
   * an English teacher fresh out of college, who wears thick glasses and has a passion for Shakespeare
   * a gym teacher who gets out on the field and runs around with the kids, cheering for them
   * a history teacher who cracks jokes and takes the students to re-enactments, but surprises them with pop quizzes and grades hard

4. One of your character's parents stays home while the other works. How does your character feel about this? Does she like coming home to a parent waiting to hear all about her day? Does she sometimes feel smothered? Does she wonder what the stay-at-home parent does while she's at school?

---

each of them will let her get away with, what punishments they mete out, or whether or not they listen to her. Some characters will have even more relatives they feel strongly about, starting with siblings. Your characters may also have aunts, uncles, cousins, grandparents or even great-grandparents, and will form opinions about them based on whether or not they're cheek-pinchers, what sorts of presents they give, how their perfume or aftershave smells or what questions they ask when they come to visit.

 Read the Pros

1. Read *Walk Two Moons* by Sharon Creech. In the beginning, Sal has very firm opinions about her momma and about her father's friend, the red-headed Margaret Cadaver. Note the way her thoughts emerge in the course of her story and how they change.

2. Read *Building Blocks* by Cynthia Voigt. Brann thinks his father is a loser, until he travels back in time to his father's childhood and finds himself face to face with his father—and his father's parents. See the way his thoughts about family change.

3. Read *The Music of Dolphins* by Karen Hesse. The first-person narrator is nonverbal in the beginning. See how she struggles to learn simple language, while her inner thoughts are clearly expressed in contrasting typeface.

Characters feel

Thoughts are rational, but real people aren't always rational, especially in tense situations. In addition to thinking with their heads, kids feel with their hearts—or their stomachs, or wherever you want their deepest emotions to come from. They fear, they get angry, they hate, they love and they feel overwhelming delight. Kids feel other emotions, too—they're curious, they may feel guilty, they may be jealous of a friend or an enemy, they get embarrassed, they feel lonely. And they pass through the spectrum of these emotions every day.

Your characters should experience a wide range of natural emotions as they live through the experiences in your story. But expressing believable emotions is more than a matter of opening your thesaurus to look up new words to describe a particular feeling. While you can articulate your character's thoughts with words, emotions are more subtle. You can evoke them in your reader by using physical sensations that the reader will recognize. The catch: You need to find a unique, quirky way to express an emotion believably, and it should spring from the context of your character.

For example, if you write that Kassie felt heat flood into her face in her embarrassment at saying something stupid to Anastasia, the most popular girl in class, the reader will recognize that flush of embarrassment, but won't really feel it. The description is overdone. You need to know a little more about your character and her situation to make the feeling strong and true, so that it will resonate for the reader.

Perhaps Kassie is an artist and knows nothing about volleyball, and Anastasia is the captain of the winning volleyball team. Kassie has said something stupid about the last game and Anastasia has withered her with a scathing reply. Instead of merely wishing the incident had never happened, artist Kassie might wish she could splash turpentine across the last half hour and repaint her life. A different kid might wish she could hit rewind on her life and record a different conversation.

By using specific sensations and reactions to express your character's emotions, you'll bring the scene to life for the reader. And, since each character is unique, the expression of his or her emotions should be unique. If you find yourself writing an emotional cliché, look for a different way to express the same idea. Instead of writing the familiar sensation of a heart "pounding in fear," your football player leaping for the reception could think of the defensive players waiting to tackle him. He doesn't just catch the ball—he crushes it to his chest so that he feels the ball pulsing wildly against his hands as he dreads its being ripped from him.

What is the reason behind the feeling?

Examine why your character feels the emotion. A small child who acts curious may feel a sense of wonder at a butterfly and want to know all about it . . . or he may want to irritate his mother so he plies Mom with questions about the butterfly to get her attention. A third grader who's jealous of a friend's new bike may feel angry at his parents for not buying him one, even if he understands that they can't afford it, and may take out his bitterness on his friend for having this prized possession.

Emotions may not always be clear in your character's mind. When her father doesn't come to kiss her goodnight for the third night in a row, Shona may throw a china nightlight that he gave her across her bedroom. Then, later, she'll creep out to pick up the pieces and use school glue to put them back together. Characters often feel a muddle of emotions or act out in one emotional language (here, Shona uses the emotional language of anger, hurling a breakable item across a room) to mask the real emotion (her fear that he doesn't love her anymore and her desperation to hold on to the security of his love).

Also remember that your character may feel one thing at one point in your story and feel a different emotion at another point. Kids are complex, and they bounce from emotional high to emotional low. Trust your characters enough to let them do this, but constantly ask yourself whether the variety of emotions rings true. Can you remember feeling those mood swings from your own childhood? Have you seen it in your children or in a friend's children? From the jumble of believable emotions, let a pattern emerge that shows a character's progress from the beginning of your story through to the end. If you use specific details to show these emotions in your characters, readers will take the boys and girls of your imagination into their hearts and will care deeply about what happens to them.

 Read the Pros

1. Read *The Keeper* by Phyllis Reynolds Naylor. As Nick tries to cope with his father's schizophrenia, see how his emotions run through a complex range, including confusion, fear, anger, resentment, embarrassment and guilt.

TRY IT YOURSELF: CHARACTERS FEEL

1. Make a list of emotions a character might feel. Next to each emotion, write a situation that might cause that emotion. Then write a physical sensation unique to the emotion that will make the reader understand how the character feels. For example, fear might be caused by the sight of a barking dog that's not on a leash. Perhaps the character feels paralyzed like a helpless china kitten, about to be crushed by monster jaws.
2. Choose one or more of those emotions from your list, and write a scene in which a youngster feels that emotion and expresses it.

---

2. Read *Beloved Benjamin Is Waiting* by Jean Karl, and see how Karl shows Lucinda's tension, confusion and fear over her parents' fights, and her helplessness when they both walk out, and she has to hide in a cemetery.
3. Read *The Language of Goldfish* by Zibby Oneal. Note the way Carrie's emotions mire her in childhood, and prevent her from accepting that she has to change and grow mentally and emotionally as she grows physically into adolescence.

Characters speak

What your character does and thinks and feels only reflects part of her personality. Kids also talk, and what they say (and how they say it) reveals a lot about their character. For readers to believe in your characters, however, you must use language appropriate to that youngster's age and circumstance. That last sentence, for example, is not something a youngster would say, and a conversation in which a child character said it wouldn't ring true to a reader. A kid might say, "If you want kids to believe in your characters, they have to sound like real kids." In other words, you need to use natural kid language.

You can get a feel for natural kid talk by listening to real children. Listen in on kids talking to each other at a fast-food restaurant or at the park. If you don't have children of your own handy, you'll find some tips for watching and listening to kids in chapter 3. Pay attention to their syntax and vocabulary, and use these in your story dialogue. But fictional conversations shouldn't exactly reproduce the "uhs," "wells," "ums" and repetitions of real speech. These don't bother the listener in real life, but they will irritate an impatient reader who wants the dialogue to move along quickly.

Kids tend to use slang. While you want your dialogue to sound contemporary, avoid using the latest slang on the block, because slang is transitory and geographically based. Since it may take six months to a year for a magazine story to see print and several years for a book to be published, any real slang you try to use will be hopelessly dated by the time kids read the conversation. If you want your characters to use slang, stick to familiar words that have been around long enough that everybody understands them, like "cool," or you can make up your own. Slang evolves from kids arbitrarily changing words or twisting figures of speech into phrases that only the in-crowd can understand. You can create this effect by making up your own words and letting the context make them clear to the reader.

Kids also mispronounce a lot of words. They may be in a hurry and run words together, like "gonna" or "wanna." Or they may drop the final "g" of a word, such as "goin'." Small children may try to use big words they can't quite pronounce yet—adults often find these mispronunciations hilarious, but children know what they mean, and they resent the grown-ups' laughter at their expense. In writing your dialogue, try not to rely too heavily on phonetic misspelling to sound like a child, or you'll alienate your readers by coming across as condescending. It's almost like an insulting dialect, as if you're telling kids that they come from an alien place and speak a strange almost-English. Respect your reader by using this technique carefully. In moderation, it can help differentiate between characters of different ages or who live in different places, but only in moderation.

Personality in dialogue

Each of your characters should sound distinct, since his voice springs from his personality. But that distinct tone should come from a character's thoughts and feelings, not solely from how he speaks. Watch out for placing too much emphasis on your characters' tag lines:

"I didn't do it," he muttered.
"You certainly did," she retorted sharply.
"But it wasn't me," he blurted loudly.
"I saw you running," she insisted firmly.
"I was chasing him!" he cried helplessly.
"Don't make matters worse by blaming someone else," she chided.
"I didn't do it," he repeated.

That scene is full of tension, but you can't tell much about the characters from their argument. Awkward tag lines with inappropriate descrip-

16

tions of the speech (like 'blurted') or weak adverbs draw the reader's attention away from what's being said to the way the character is saying it. That ends up being distracting. You can show your character more clearly by using simple tags (such as "said" or "told" or "asked") blended with action sentences which show us more about the speaker:

"I didn't do it," the boy said, staring at the school yard ground.

"You certainly did," said the yard teacher.

"But it wasn't me." The boy looked up at her, his eyes intense under tangled hair that needed cutting.

"I saw you running," she told him. But she frowned, as if trying to remember exactly what she had seen.

"I was chasing him!" the boy cried. He flung his arms wide to show he had no lies up his sleeves.

At his gesture, the teacher folded her own arms and glared at him. "Don't make matters worse by blaming someone else."

The boy's arms fell to his sides. He slumped, staring at the cracked concrete again. "I didn't do it," he said in a voice so low the yard teacher leaned forward to make out the words.

Even though you still don't know what the boy is accused of, these two characters begin to come into focus so the reader can care about them. The tension comes from wondering which one to believe.

Nothing but the truth?

Kids (and adults, for that matter) don't always tell the truth, especially when they're speaking to each other. A parent or a teacher may simplify something, thinking the child couldn't possibly understand. The adult might even lie deliberately, not wanting to frighten the child. But kids often sense that sort of untruth. Use the tension between what your characters say and what they know to be true to illuminate their personalities and their thoughts for your reader.

Kids can lie to each other, too. They may be bragging and their imagination just takes over, or they may choose to deliberately mislead a friend or an enemy. Or they may simply fail to say exactly what they mean, and the other kid misunderstands. Some characters may immediately set their friends straight, while others may not realize a misunderstanding has taken root. And some might decide to let the other kid keep the wrong interpretation, justifying it to themselves because it's the other's fault, not their own.

Kids can also lie to their parents or teachers to avoid getting punished or to protect the adult from the truth. In that situation, you can explore the way a character feels about deceiving someone he loves or admires. Whether a youngster tells an adult the truth or not, she'll sound different talking to a teacher or a minister or a parent than she'll sound talking to her friends. Kids won't use the same slang talking to adults, for instance, unless they deliberately want to confuse them. A youngster may be more polite when he's talking to an adult. He may deliberately try to use complete sentences, while he might talk to his friends in phrases. Another kid may become monosyllabic, especially in front of an adult he doesn't know.

Pieces of the puzzle

As you develop your characters, trust them to let you know how they feel about a situation, and use their dialogue as well as their thoughts and actions to express their feelings. Believable kids act, think, feel and speak. These are pieces of the puzzle that will make up a whole character. Now you need to find ways to think like a youngster and feel like a youngster to breathe life into your child characters.

Read the Pros

1. Read the opening chapters in *The Master Puppeteer* by Katherine Paterson. Pay attention to the way the ritual courteous dialogue between Jiro's father and Mochida masks what each of them mean until Jiro speaks up. Note the difference in the conversations between his parents when Jiro is present, and the one he overhears at the end of chapter 2.

2. Read *Beloved Benjamin Is Waiting* by Jean Karl. See how the dialogue between Joel and Lucinda in the epilogue works even though Karl doesn't include any thoughts or emotions or action, because the reader knows Lucinda so well by the end of the book.

3. For an example of original slang, read *Alien Secrets* by Annette Curtis Klause. See how Puck's slang becomes clear to the reader by the context.

4. Read *Nothing but the Truth* by Avi. Look at the way the characters' separate perceptions of an event force the reader to draw his own conclusions about it. You can find another example of this technique in *The Child Buyer*, by John Hersey.

TRY IT YOURSELF: CHARACTERS SPEAK

1. Write a conversation between two characters without any tag lines or action. Choose a particular situation: two boys waiting to be picked for soccer teams, a small child talking with an older sibling, two girls shopping at the mall. This will be all dialogue, like the epilogue in *Beloved Benjamin Is Waiting*.

2. Now write the same conversation, choosing one character to be your main character and adding in that character's thoughts and feelings.

3. Rewrite the scene again, using the main character's thoughts and feelings along with the dialogue, and add in the action. Show each character as he or she moves or gestures. Use facial expressions to reflect their feelings. Your characters are the sum of what they do, what they think, what they feel and what they say. Hold on to this scene—in Part II, you'll see how to take characters like these and craft a story around them.

REMEMBER THE CHILD YOU WERE

Creating a Character Journal

It's probably been a long time since you were growing up. You may feel daunted at the thought of turning back the calendar and thinking like a kid again. Don't worry—being a child is a lot like riding a bicycle. Once you experience it, you know all about the emotions and thoughts of childhood, and you never really forget. You just have to draw the memories out of the depths of the adult you've become, and use them to inspire your stories and books for children. A good story shows a young character's path through the mysteries of self-discovery—usually because the writer has struggled down that path of self-discovery himself.

Finding your memories

The first step is to find the memories that hold the potential for strong character personalities and traits. If you kept a journal or diary when you were a child, you can re-read it to bring those days back into focus. As you read, look for incidents that strike a chord, and jot them down.

Get some sort of notebook in which you can explore your memories in order to create characters—something you can carry around with you, if possible. Or you can set up a file in your computer if you prefer composing at the keyboard. This character journal isn't for anyone else to see. It's for freewriting about memories and for brainstorming answers to questions that will trigger memories. A blank page in your character journal can invite you to find your way into these memories. Let your mind wander through events in your childhood that you recorded in diaries, through the stories your old friends and your parents tell you, and through stories you've heard for the umpteenth time at family reunions.

Certain incidents will trigger strong reactions from you—a wince, a smile or a flush you remember all too well, as if it were happening all over again. When this occurs, don't question why you're drawn to that incident—just jot it down in your character journal. Close your eyes and drift through the past, not searching, just remembering. When a memory grabs your attention, write it down.

Once you've made your list, look it over and see if one incident seems to reach out to you. At different moments in our lives, certain memories carry greater significance than others do, based on what we're going through at the time. So go with the one that moves you now, but save the others for later.

Freewrite about the event as it plays itself out in your mind. Go for as many specific details as you can—descriptive details about who is with you; what you see, hear and smell around you; and how you feel about the incident. Don't worry about punctuation or grammar or spelling. Write in fragments if you like. What's important is that you capture the event and your feelings about it and get that down on paper. The "you" you're writing about carries the heart of a character kids will be able to relate to.

Identifying memories that will motivate characters

As you read your diaries and journals, those moments that trigger reactions carry the potential for stories.

⋆ Look for moments when you were brave. Stop and think about them. Did you know you had that courage in you, or did it surprise you at the time? A young character who becomes an unexpected hero might feel this way. Look also for moments when you were afraid. Were there places, or other kids, or even adults that made you afraid? Why did these places or people frighten you? How did you act out when you were angry? What did you do when you were happy? Did you share your delight with other kids, or keep it to yourself and your diary?

⋆ Recall the activities you enjoyed—and those you didn't. What games did you play for fun? Why did you like them? Was it the game itself, the kids you played with or where you were playing?

Think about the games the other kids played that you didn't like. Was it the games you disliked or the kids who played them? What books did you like to read? Think about why they unlocked your deepest feelings.

★ Perhaps you had a pet—a playful dog; a cat who sat on your lap while you read, or while you wrote in your journal, or while you cried; a horse you rode; or chickens you fed. Remember what it was about this creature that made you able to trust it and perhaps even confide in it. Or perhaps you had an imaginary friend or an imaginary pet who understood everything about you. Your characters may have imaginary companions, also. Use your own to inspire these.

★ You probably had a favorite ring or some other charm you wore or carried for luck. Did your friends understand, or did they tease you about it? Remember when you lost something that broke your heart. What was it? Why was it so precious? Did your friends sympathize or think you were crazy? Your characters may have their own talismans—and they will have friends, some of whom will understand, and some who won't. As these different memories come into focus for you, jot them down in your character journal. You can build on them to develop story characters.

A diary can be a terrific way to rediscover the agonies and delights of growing up. Unfortunately, not all of us knew then that we'd grow up to be writers or that the heartbreaks and joys of childhood would one day be important to us again. But the mind is a wonderful thing. There are all sorts of treasures locked inside it, and it's just waiting for you to ask to see them. The first thing to try is closing your eyes and letting your mind drift as you explore any one of these memory questions about significant moments, activities or friends while you were growing up. Then you can freewrite about the answers to these questions in your character journal.

Read the Pros

1. Read *One of the Third Grade Thonkers* by Phyllis Reynolds Naylor. See how Naylor develops Jimmy and his friends as characters to explore what real courage means to kids.

2. Read *The Fastest Friend in the West* by Vicki Grove. See how Grove shows the characters of Lori and Vern. They're both lonely kids, but each girl has a very different secret that will bind them into a friendship that changes them both.

TRY IT YOURSELF: FIND YOUR MEMORIES

You can transform the people you remember from childhood into characters to use in your writing. Probe your memories for people—other kids and adults both. Use these questions to help you explore your memories. Think about the person and recall a specific incident involving him or her, then write about it in your character journal.

1. Who did you admire most around your neighborhood or at school? Why?
2. How did you show your admiration for these heroes?
3. Can you remember a new kid who was put in your class? What was the kid like? How did you react?
4. Did you ever move as a kid, so you were the new kid in school? How did you feel? How did the other kids treat you?
5. Who did you mistrust or fear? Why?
6. Was there ever someone you lied to instinctively? Why?
7. Who could you always turn to for help and advice? Why did you choose that person?
8. What trendy outfit or bike or toy did you long for? Which kid did you envy, who already had this cherished item? How did you feel about that kid? Did you ever get that item you coveted? Was it as good in reality as the dream had been?

Memory keys

But what if you didn't keep a diary and your mind is a complete blank? Tangible objects can work like keys to unlock your memories. If your parents were pack rats who kept everything (perhaps they knew you were going to be a writer, even if you didn't!), go home for a visit and dig through boxes of your old school papers and class pictures. Remember just how important the world of school was when you were growing up, and use your agonies and achievements to make kids you remember from the classroom come alive for your readers.

Think back to first grade. Who was your buddy, the one you were irrevocably paired with in line? Did your heart sink or leap when the teacher announced your buddy's name? Did you ride the school bus to school? How did it feel to climb on the bus for the first time? Where did you sit? Who sat next to you? Did the two of you become friends or enemies? Were you well behaved on the bus, or were you a troublemaker?

Try to prevent your memories from being sanitized or superficial—recall the specific details of the scene, the other kids and your feelings about the incident.

Perhaps you walked to school. What stands out in your memory about that walk? Remember what you saw and heard, and what frightened you along the way. Did you walk alone, or with an older sibling or parent? How old were you when you got to walk to school with your friends? What was the ritual you followed to meet up together each morning? Your characters will have to get to school if your story is set during the school year, and the more clearly you can remember yourself and your friends in the same situation, the more believably you'll write the scene.

School friends

Try to remember a time when your best friend let you down in front of the whole class. Can you still remember the details of the betrayal? Write about the incident in your character journal. Was that the end of your friendship, or did you get over it? Were things really ever the same?

Also remember a time when your best friend was the only one who stood by you. How did you feel—thankful, or ashamed no one else stood up for you? Or were you embarrassed because you were afraid you wouldn't have done the same? Were you ever able to show your friend how you felt about that loyalty? The bonds and constraints of friendship will be a natural part of any book or story you write, so dig deep in your memory to discover specific incidents that will resonate with your readers.

In addition to other kids, remember your teachers. Who was your favorite teacher? Why? Which teacher did you strive to please, only to fail? How? Did you ever understand why? Which teacher always expected a little more of you than you thought you could manage? Did you come through? How did you celebrate your achievement? Or how did you deal with your sense of failure?

Think about your secrets from school days. Did anyone ever catch you cheating? Why were you doing it? How were you punished? Did you ever get away with cheating? How did you feel after that? Did you ever lie to a teacher about something you'd done or something a friend did? Did the teacher believe you, or were you caught?

Other people's evidence

These details of the kids and teachers who peopled your school life will allow you to populate your own school stories with believable characters who readers will recognize. If you're having trouble remembering the faces from your school pictures and the details of your school highs and lows, try probing other people's memories. Are you still close to your

TRY IT YOURSELF: MEMORY KEYS

School memories offer great inspiration for stories. Once kids start first grade, they spend seven hours a day in school and several more hours riding school buses, playing with school friends and doing school homework. While your feelings about school and your experiences there will ring true for today's kids, school itself has changed. Spend some time researching your child's school or the school your friends' children attend.

1. Talk to the teachers.
   * What subjects do they teach in each grade?
   * How much homework do they assign?
   * What supplies do the kids use? Do the kids bring their own supplies, or is each family required to contribute supplies to a communal supply center, so the kids can take what they need?
2. Walk through the halls.
   * What class projects hang on the walls?
   * How big are the student lockers? What color and condition? Is a locker still big enough to stuff a kid into? What do kids stash in their lockers besides books and jackets?
   * Do kids carry their books in their arms, in book bags or sports bags, or in backpacks?
3. Talk to people in the school office.
   * Is there a school dress code?
   * What conduct will earn a visit to the principal's office?
   * What behavior will keep students off of the school buses? For how long?
   * What will earn detention, suspension or even expulsion?
4. Ask about the school yard.
   * What's the recess schedule?
   * What do students do on stormy days or in the winter if there's snow?
   * What games do the kids play?
   * How many teachers are on yard duty? What do they do?
5. Check out the cafeteria.
   * What's on the menu? (Many schools these days offer salad bars in addition to hot cafeteria food.)
   * Does the school have a free meal program? How do the kids qualify? Do all the kids know who's in the program?
   * Do lots of kids bring their own lunches or do most seem to buy?
   * What's inside some of the bag lunches kids bring themselves?

best friends from grade school? Spend a late night reminiscing—a grown-up version of those remembered sleep overs. As your friends relate personal impressions of your shared school experiences, their stories will trigger your own memories of the same events.

Don't be surprised if your first reaction is, "That's not the way it was at all!" Two people rarely see anything exactly the same way. You don't have to agree with anyone else's interpretation of your experience, but listening to the way someone else remembers it can help remind you of how you felt at the time. Don't argue—but don't feel compelled to be fair to everyone else who was involved when you write about the incident after your friends are gone.

 Read the Pros

1. Read *There's a Boy in the Girls' Bathroom* by Louis Sachar. Note the way Sachar shows Bradley's and Jeff's individual weaknesses and strengths, then shows how they are exacerbated by the boys' experiences in school.
2. For a different twist on school stories, read *Witch Week* by Diana Wynne Jones, *Wizard's Hall* by Jane Yolen or *Harry Potter and the Sorcerer's Stone* by J.K. Rowling. The teachers, classmates and school world of bells, classes, homework and detention in these magic-filled fantasies are all taken from familiar school life that readers will recognize.
3. Read *Keep Ms. Sugarman in the Fourth Grade* by Elizabeth Levy. Teachers can be as important as best friends. A good teacher matters deeply to Jackie in this book. Be sure to read Levy's dedication note to the real Ms. Sugarman and her author's note about her memories of this special teacher in her biographical material.

Take good notes in one section of your character journal. Many of these answers may differ from school to school, however. If you set your story in your hometown, then whatever your school does is the norm for your book. But if you deliberately set a story in a different town, do some research there to see how things are done.

Family memories

Kids spend a lot of time thinking about school, but they also go home and have to deal with their parents, brothers and sisters, and extended family members. You probably commented on your family (or complained about them) in your diary or talked about them to your friends. If your parents live in the same house or apartment you grew up in, look around next time you visit. Remember your room and how you felt sitting in it with your door closed. Remember the comics you'd slip under the mattress when you heard your mother's footsteps in the hallway. Remember how it felt to sneak out to the refrigerator after you were sure your parents were asleep—your toes curling at the chilly linoleum on the kitchen floor, your hand reaching into the freezer for the ice cream, and the creak of the floorboards in the hallway that said you weren't the only person awake after all.

Remember the bustle to get ready for school in the morning. Did you have to wait in line for the bathroom, or were there enough bathrooms in your house? How many siblings did you have? Did you have a room to yourself, or did you have to share? Did you have a favorite sibling? Why? Did you have a sibling who picked on you? How did you feel about that sibling? Did you long to please him or her, or did you resent him or her? Did you pick on one of your siblings? Why? Did you ever feel guilty about it, or did you feel glad to be the one on top?

Were you the oldest, the youngest or in the middle? Did you like your position in the family, or did you wish you were older or younger? Why? Think carefully about your relationships with your siblings. It's not enough to write:

> I had an older brother and a younger sister. They were OK. My older brother wore glasses and read a lot and didn't have much time for me. My little sister played with dolls until she discovered makeup. I guess we didn't have a lot in common.

Instead, really stop and think about them as people:

> I had an older brother and a younger sister. Why couldn't I have been the oldest, just for a day? My big brother never let us forget he was the oldest! He'd stand there, cleaning his glasses on his shirttail, telling us to bring in the trash cans or fold the laundry because he was busy. When I complained, he told Mom he was studying and held up a really thick book. No one had opened that book since I was born—he'd really been reading science fiction magazines. But Mom always said, "Let him study!" He grew up to be a lawyer. I don't see much of him.
>
> My little sister—well, talk about a spoiled brat! The baby of the family. Why couldn't they have stopped with me? If I couldn't be the oldest, being the baby wouldn't have been so bad. She had a room to herself, no sharing. And all those dolls—all those faces

28

staring at you when you walked in! She talked to them and giggled with them. It was disgusting. No wonder none of us ever talked to her, except when Mom made one of us take charge of her when we were going somewhere. Then she got older and discovered makeup and boys. You'd think they were something new, as if she hadn't grown up with a family full of them!

I'd forgotten how much I felt like an alien in my own family, as if I'd come from another planet. I used to go up on the roof and sit there and look at the stars and wish someone would come and take me away—until my sister found out and dragged Mom up the access ladder, and Mom nearly had a heart attack when she saw me there. I wasn't allowed to go up on the roof ever again.

The extra details open up all sorts of possible story lines you could explore with characters inspired by your siblings—or storylines inspired by your own feelings of alienation. If you make yourself remember in detail, you'll surprise yourself with insights you didn't have then and emotions you'd forgotten. Use these memories of sibling relationships to create fictional families in your stories.

Recalling parents

Your characters will have parents as well as siblings. To show them through your characters' eyes, spend some time recalling your own parents as you knew them as a child. Think about each parent, including stepparents if you had them or missing or deceased parents if you grew up in a one-parent household. Ask yourself:

* Did a parent fix breakfast for you, or did you have to fend for yourself?
* Did both your parents work? Was one a stay-at-home parent? Was one out of work? Were they on welfare?
* Did you have only one parent?
* When you got home from school, was anyone at home? How did you feel about coming home to an empty house? Or a crowded house?
* What did you admire about each of your parents? What did you dislike?
* Was there anything about one of your parents that frightened you? What?
* Did you want to be just like your parents? Why? Did that change as you grew from preschool through elementary school and middle school?

If your family has photo albums or scrapbooks, look through the pages at family members participating in various events. Do they look the way you remember them? Watch yourself grow up through the camera's eye. Look at the way the photo frames the moment. Can you remember how you felt when the shutter clicked? Recall what was going on. Was it a special family event at which you were having a miserable time? What would you rather have been doing? Or was it a perfect afternoon? Why? Did you have a special secret in the back of your mind that made you smile that way? What was it? Did you have a problem that worried you while everyone else was smiling? What?

Also take the time to talk with your parents, and ask them about their memories of your family while you were growing up. Just like your school friends, they'll probably have a different take on events than you remember, but they may also shed light on impressions that were vague in your mind. Listen to what they say, but also watch them as they talk, and remember how you saw them as a child. They were bigger then, for one thing, and at different times you either hung on their every word or doubted everything they said. Probably your most potent memories come from that childhood connection with your parents.

 Read the Pros

1. Read *Dicey's Song* by Cynthia Voigt, and see how Voigt explores the latticework of relationships between the members of the Tillerman family.
2. Read *The Secret in Miranda's Closet* by Sheila Greenwald. Miranda and her mother each have very firm opinions about the other, but when Miranda's secret is exposed they're both in for some surprises.
3. Read *Save Halloween!* by Stephanie S. Tolen. Johnna's family struggles not to split apart under pressure when her parents and brothers end up caught in the middle between Johnna's class Halloween pageant and her uncle's crusade to abolish "Satan's own holiday."

Stories from your extended family

In addition to your own life, you can draw on the lives of the people around you—your parents, grandparents, brothers and sisters, cousins. Listen at family weddings and reunions, and ask questions to get your relatives talking—questions about their relationships with other family members and questions about their memories of growing up. Look for answers that generate an echo in you.

My father's family comes from El Salvador, and most of my relatives

TRY IT YOURSELF: FAMILY MEMORIES, PART I

1. Write at least one specific memory about one of your siblings in your character journal. If you were an only child, remember the differences between your solitary condition and your friends who had siblings. How did you feel about those differences? Write in your character journal about at least one specific instance when you either envied your friends because of their siblings or were abjectly thankful that you were an only child.

2. Remember the way you saw your parents when you were young. Write about at least one specific instance when you felt a strong surge of admiration, love, fear or hatred for one of your parents in your character journal.

3. If you can look through a family photo album or scrapbook, choose one photograph and write about your memories of that event in your character journal. After you've written your impression, ask someone else who was in the photograph if they remember that instance. Write down that person's account and compare the two versions.

on that side still live in El Salvador. While the guerrilla war was being fought in the 1980s, I was concerned for them. My grandmother's letters told a fascinating and disturbing tale of how life went on in spite of the fighting on the sidewalk right outside the family home and in the streets between my cousins' home and where they went to school. The images stayed with me and ultimately became *A Bear for Miguel*.

I'm also a teddy bear collector, which may seem irrelevant to the war in El Salvador, but I brought the two ideas together in the person of a young girl who goes to market with her Papa, taking her cherished teddy bear. In the beginning, Maria is excited about the trip, until she realizes they have no money to buy food. Because of the war, Papa can't work for the government factory or the guerrillas might punish him, and he can't work for the men who support the guerrillas or the army might arrest him, so they have to trade things for food. Maria wants to help her family, and when Papa leaves her alone briefly, Maria sees her chance. When a nice couple comes up and is interested in trading, she's sure she's going to get the milk for the baby at home—but then they see her bear, and they are willing to trade all they have to get Maria's teddy bear for their little boy who was crippled in the fighting.

TRY IT YOURSELF: FAMILY MEMORIES, PART II

Below, you'll find some starter questions you can ask family members at reunions and get-togethers. Maybe some of your relatives' answers will evoke empathy from you, and you'll identify with the teller. Write down their stories in your journal, and use them.

1. What games did you play when you were growing up?
2. Who was your best friend? Why did you like him or her? Did you ever fight with your best friend? Why?
3. Who was the meanest kid around? What did he or she do to you?
4. What was your school like? How did you like your teachers?
5. Did you walk to school, ride a school bus or take a public bus or subway? How long did it take to get to school in the morning?
6. Did you ever do something you weren't supposed to when you were a kid? What happened?
7. Did you have a pet?
8. Did your parents work? How did you feel about coming home to an empty house? Or did you stay with friends or family? How did you like that?
9. Did you fight with your brothers or sisters? Why? Did you ever team up with your brothers or sisters to fight an outsider? What happened?

I drew on a lot for this book—my grandmother's letters, my love of my own childhood teddy bears and family memories. In my character journal, I had written about my parents arguing about money when I was small, and I used this in the book to show how difficult times can make parents cross and tense. I also remembered how my father would try to laugh and make a joke out of everything, even problems, and how it irritated my mother. I didn't know what to think then, but now I know that joking was his way of keeping misery at bay. In the book, Maria's papa also laughs in the face of disaster to try to keep it from hurting the family he loves.

You can mix your own memories with family stories in the same way. Listen at family gatherings for the familiar stories that rend your heart or make you laugh. These stories that belong to your family belong to you as well, and you can use the characters and the feelings in a family story that resonates for you.

Characters you know

Experienced writers often give this advice: *Write what you know.*

It sounds so simple, but the immediate response most people have to that is: *What do I know? My life's so ordinary.* Making the transition from what you know to writing strong books and stories lies in realizing just how extraordinary your life is. No one else has lived your experiences or has seen what you have seen through your perspective. The ultimate resource you have to draw on as a writer is yourself—your heart, your hopes, your secret fears, your joys and your despairs. And "write what you know" is your best advice in creating strong child characters, because you know so much about being a child. You just have to rediscover your childhood memories.

The next time you hear "write what you know," don't groan and go blank. Instead, head for your character journal. Forget writer's block. You never have to worry about running out of new ideas—your life is full of experiences that you feel strongly about. And when your fiction and nonfiction is born from real griefs and delights that you have worked through and transcended, readers will recognize themselves in your characters. Your memories will live forever through your readers, and your transformation of your yesterdays into stories and articles for today will inspire young readers to face their tomorrows.

 Read the Pros

1. Read other author biographies and look for links between their childhood memories and the books and stories they write. Try *Lois Lowry* and *Avi* by Lois Markham.

2. In addition to writing stories for their young fans, many writers write about their own lives. Read autobiographies of the authors whose books you enjoy, looking for incidents from their lives that inspired scenes in their books. You might try *26 Fairmont Avenue* by Tomie dePaola; *How I Came to Be a Writer* by Phyllis Reynolds Naylor; *Author: A True Story* by Helen Lester; *Boy: Tales of Childhood* by Roald Dahl and its sequel, *Going Solo; The Abracadabra Kid: A Writer's Life* by Sid Fleischman; *Anonymously Yours* by Richard Peck; and *But I'll Be Back Again* by Cynthia Rylant.

TRY IT YOURSELF: CHARACTERS YOU KNOW

1. Use any of these idea generators to freewrite a memory in your character journal:
   * ☆ diary entries
   * ☆ school pictures and class papers
   * ☆ recollections of an old school friend
   * ☆ memories of siblings and parents
   * ☆ family photo albums
   * ☆ parents' reminiscences
   * ☆ family reunions

   Describe what happened and what you did. Write about how you felt. Don't gloss over your emotions. Be as explicit and honest as you can, even if your feelings weren't especially admirable. Make notes on who else was involved and what they did. Write down what you wish they had done. Write down what you wish you had done differently.

2. Think about that memory for a while. Step back from it and think about what happened with the understanding you now have as an adult. What impact did the incident have on you? How did it change you as a person? Or did someone else involved in the incident change as a result? How did you feel about that then? How do you feel about it now? Try to express in your journal the way this event changed you and helped you grow up.

3. Once you've recaptured your feelings about this incident and identified its significance, think some more about the other people involved and how they felt. Observing real people outside of yourself is another way to create believable story characters.

SEE DICK AND JANE

Observing Real Kids

Remembering your own childhood is a great way to capture emotions and feelings, but kids in the twenty-first century have experiences we can hardly imagine. Surely we never whizzed down busy streets the way kids do today on their in-line skates. Think back. Were your old, scuffed roller skates ever as swift as you scraped down cracked and pebbled concrete sidewalks, a chill metal skate key banging against your heaving chest? You can recall the triumph of winning a ball game or setting a track record, but can you know the exhilaration of setting a record on the latest Nintendo game? You can still feel the anguish of losing a best friend to the new kid in class, but can you envision a city kid slouching into a rural sixth-grade classroom with one side of his head shaved, wearing seven earrings and two nose rings?

Kids reading your books and stories will expect to meet contemporary characters like this. Unless you intend to limit yourself to writing historical fiction, you'll need to share these experiences yourself so you can pass them on to your characters. To do this you must observe today's children and learn to put yourself in their places, thinking their thoughts and experiencing their emotional highs and lows.

Children around you

If you're a teacher or a professional who works with children in another capacity, you're around contemporary children a lot and you probably have a good understanding of them. If you're a parent or grandparent, you get shopping lists from your family for the latest toys, and you can see your pint-sized relatives in action in your backyard, family room or driveway. You take them to get their hair cut, and you refuse to give permission for body piercing or tattoos until they're at least thirteen. So you stay in touch with contemporary children. Chances are you even find yourself carpooling the kids to activities where you can watch them interact with other youngsters.

But your observation can be clouded by your sense of parental responsibility. Parents have the urge to nurture their little darlings, or more realistically, to train their children to be well-behaved credits to them, especially in public. Give yourself a holiday and have some fun with your children, rather than trying to be responsible all the time. Rationalize that you're being responsible to your writing instead of your parenting for a few hours. Your children won't suffer.

Take time to play with them as an equal. Before you yell "Stop!" ask yourself why they did whatever upset you. Put yourself in the same position. When you were two, why did you lie on top of the party balloon until it burst? Did you like the bouncy feeling against your stomach? Did you know it would explode? Once you got over the surprise (and maybe even the fright), was the fun of bouncing on the balloon worth the noise of the explosion and the feeling of splatting down on the floor?

If you can't remember your kid logic from long ago, let your children show you how it's done. While they play, try to follow your children's reasoning. Let them argue over who gets to play with the truck next, rather than wading in and settling the debate. Listen to their logic. Your characters of the same age should reason in the same way.

Writers who are single, childless or have long since raised their kids and seen them move away have even more difficulty imagining what it's like to be a child in the twenty-first century. What's the solution? You can watch children's television to get a sense of their interests and what they're wearing, but that's an artificial medium. You may have no intention of having babies of your own, and adoption could be out of the question. Sneaking through a mall trailing a group of adolescents might put a security guard on your tail. And sitting surreptitiously in a park watching other people's children and taking notes could get you arrested by wary parents or baby-sitters. But there are alternatives.

Play with kids

You probably know someone who has children. Volunteer to take charge of the kids for an afternoon. Ask the kids what they want to do, and do it with them. Take two or three youngsters to the zoo or the video arcade or a museum or the pool. It will give you a chance to see kids interacting and listen to them talking. You might even bring along a microcassette recorder in your pocket and tape their conversation. Don't worry about parenting. Just keep them safe and share their fun. It's a chance to be a kid yourself for a little while. Expect to feel exhausted, but also expect to start bringing contemporary kid qualities into focus in your characters.

If you're not brave enough to take the kids out on your own, ask your friends to let you hang around the house and play with their children. Promise your friends you won't let any disaster befall their offspring, and then forget about being an adult and just play. Soar on the swing set in the backyard with the preschoolers. Play board games or balance on a skateboard with the primary graders. Play computer games with the middle graders. Get the kids to show you their rooms, and tell them how cool they are. Get them talking, and they'll show you the possessions they prize most, and maybe even let you see their secret hiding places. Treat these confidences with respect, and the kids may open up to you even further.

Work with kids

Another way to watch kids is to volunteer, even if you don't know the kids you'll be working with. Your church youth group might need an extra adult, or the community Girls Club or Boys Club could use adults to chaperone parties or teach classes. Area teams could need extra coaches, local Boy Scout and Girl Scout groups may need assistant leaders or your church could need more Sunday school teachers. You'll have to work instead of play, but this allows you to interact with kids in a different spirit. Many coming-of-age stories feature mentoring, so watch the way the kids look up to the adults who help them. But keep your attention primarily focused on the kids themselves at this point. In children's books and stories, adults tend to remain secondary characters since the reader most closely identifies with the youngsters.

If you remember your own unathletic school days and fear looking like a klutz on the baseball diamond, football field or basketball court, you could simply adopt a neighborhood team and regularly go to watch their practices and games. Be aware that adults worry about the kids they supervise in this day and age, however. Unknown adults who hang around children's activities without a kid of their own can be quickly labeled dangerous "strangers." If you know a parent of one of the kids on the team, explain that you'd like to watch to help you with your

TRY IT YOURSELF: OBSERVE CHILDREN AROUND YOU

Spend time with your kids, or borrow a friend's kid for the day. Afterward, find a quiet place (in your car or in the bathroom), and begin taking notes on everything you can remember about each child. Try answering these questions:

1. What was he wearing? Make detailed notes. While you're with him, ask casually whether Mom or Dad chose the clothes, or whether he did. If Mom made the choice, does he like that outfit? Why or why not?

2. What does she look like? Pay attention to details:
   * eye color and expression
   * hair color and style
   * height, especially compared to the other kids
   * weight, in terms of how she moves

3. What does she like to do? Ask her why, if you can do it naturally without making her feel interrogated. Otherwise, just see what she does, and whether she looks like she's suffering or having fun.

4. How does he handle something like a game piece? Remember the significance of action. Does he lunge forward and grab it, slip one finger forward to push it along the board or hesitate before moving it at all?

5. Notice whether she runs quickly and gracefully, or awkwardly. Look at her feet. Are they barefoot or is she wearing shoes? What type of shoe? Does she pick up her feet or scuff them along?

---

writing. Otherwise, introduce yourself to the coach and ask if it's all right for you to watch the team. Coaches may think you're strange, but at least they won't regard you as sinister.

Sports action gains its authenticity from specific detail. A kid doesn't just catch a ball. The player keeps an eye on the ball in the air and shifts her weight, then moves backward or forward or to one side to intercept the ball. If it's sunny, she may need to pull her cap down to shade her eyes, or hold her free hand up as a visor. Meanwhile her mitt will come up. If she's calculated right, the ball might slap right into her glove. Her other hand will come across to either keep the ball nestled safely in place or to grab it to throw for another out. And that's only the sequence of events when everything goes right! If the player miscalculates, she has to correct her position at the last minute, perhaps even leaping into the air. She may have to shove her cap off to see. She may miss the ball, fumble or drop it, and have to scramble to recover it. She may do any of this deftly or awkwardly.

Making careful notes of the way kids move on the field, whatever sport you're observing, will help you develop your sports characters and show them in action so that kids reading your book will believe in them and care about them. And even if you're not writing a sports story right now, your characters will walk and run and perhaps climb or bike or take some other action that will benefit from your field observations. Use the "Try it Yourself" exercises on page 40 to help you take detailed notes when you observe teams in action.

 Read the Pros

1. Read *Wrestling Sturbridge* by Rich Wallace. Note the honesty of his observation of athletes and how this makes his story more compelling.

2. Read *Bat 6* by Virginia Euwer Wolff. See how Wolff shows each girl's character through her action on the field as well as through her narration.

A kids'-eye view of characters

You can also get involved with kids in your local library. Bring some of your manuscripts or a few of your clips if you've been published, and show them to the children's librarian. Explain that you're a children's writer and would like to spend some time in the children's room observing the kids. You probably made friends with the librarian long ago, since most children's writers check out lots of children's books to read themselves, but explain that you have a special motive this time. Chances are, the librarian will be delighted to help you. You can set up shop in a corner of the children's room, sitting at a table with a pile of books camouflaging your notebook, and watch the kids as they swarm over the shelves, fight for who gets to use the computer next, read books aloud to themselves or to each other, or listen to audio books.

Once the library staff gets to know you, they may even ask you to get involved in some of the children's programs, like story hour. You'll be able to read to the kids, and find out what they like about certain books—or what they don't like! Don't hesitate to ask if they liked the characters in the book you just read them. Then ask them why, and make note of the qualities children notice.

Reading to a group of children also allows you to watch their dynam-

TRY IT YOURSELF: OBSERVE KIDS IN ACTION

1. Watch the players. Pay attention to the way they move. Are some kids awkward while others move with the grace of professional athletes? Break their motions down into separate moves, so you can describe the action on the field.

2. Watch the sidelines. Is one player a leader? How does he or she assert authority? Or do the other kids simply look to that player when there's a decision to be made?

3. Watch out for the player who always fumbles. Does this kid seem to be a clown, or is the player earnestly trying? Do mistakes seem to be the result of growth spurts (a kid tripping over too big feet, for instance), lack of athletic ability or lack of practice? (It may take you some experience to distinguish these. When you're getting started, just observe the action.)

4. Watch the way the other players interact with the kid who always goofs. Do they tease him good-naturedly, groan, call him names, ignore him kindly or freeze him out? Does one kid pick on him worse than the others? Is that a talented player or someone who fumbles almost as often? Is one of the kids nicer than the others? What does he do to encourage the inept player?

5. Watch the interaction between the kids and their coaches. How do the adults coach players who need help? Do they praise kids who are doing well? How? How do the kids react to the coaches? Do the players listen? Do they ignore the coach and keep making the same mistakes? Or do they tune out the coach and listen to parents in the stands calling out advice? If there's more than one coach, do they get along, or do they argue with each other? Does a coach connect with the kids so that they listen to him and respect him and like him, perhaps joking with him or getting hugs or pats on the shoulder? Or do the kids appear to respect the coach but not like him, acting impersonal or even avoiding physical contact?

6. Watch the people in the bleachers—parents, friends, siblings. Do they cheer for the players or call out complaints? Do they whisper among themselves, shaking their heads, even if they call out encouraging words? How do the players react when they have someone in the bleachers? Note which ones look embarrassed, which ones wave and look excited, which ones look crushed to hear criticisms, which ones correct something they're doing wrong when a parent calls out a comment.

ics. Pay attention to the way they listen and the way they shift around in their chairs or on the floor. Most adults think kids like to sit cross-legged on the floor to listen to stories—kids like to sit on the floor or on the ground outdoors when they play, but they're constantly in motion. Children sitting cross-legged on the floor during a program tend to fidget and shift position and talk to each other. Sometimes this means they're losing interest, but more often it means they're uncomfortable sitting still so long (don't you find the floor hard and uncomfortable?) or just have natural energy to burn. Watch the way they move, so you can let your characters fidget the same way.

A feast of observations

If you're not quite ready for such hands-on experiences, you can find a more impersonal way to observe children by going out to eat. If you're interested in writing about middle graders, try hanging out in a fast-food restaurant after school or sitting in a mall food court on Saturday afternoon. If you're interested in writing about preschoolers or primary graders, try an early supper at a family restaurant. Bring a thick notepad and stake out your claim on a table in the middle where you'll have a clear view of many other tables. Order a lengthy meal so you can take as long as possible.

In a fast-food restaurant, you can get several courses of small orders. It costs more than an extra value meal, but it's a bargain price to pay for a ringside seat to watch the kids. Pay attention to the way they sit in the chairs and to who they sit beside—middle graders treasure friendships. Do they share French fries, or are they possessive and territorial? If the fast-food chain has giveaways, do the kids keep them, trade them or throw them away? Middle graders are notorious collectors, but they're also very self-conscious about baby things, so some fast-food chain toys may be beneath them. This is also a terrific way to observe modern kids' clothes and physical appearances—styles have changed considerably since most writers were kids! Think of the following questions in the "Physical Appearance Checklist" when you're observing kids.

Physical Appearance Checklist

Boy or girl?

Approximate age (Do they mention what grade they're in?)

What is each kid wearing?

★ Shirt—T-shirt, sweatshirt, button-down, blouse, polo shirt, sweater, something else?

      Color: (pattern, print, weave, single color?)

      Fit: (baggy, tight, just right?)

Fabric:

Condition: (new, faded, holes?)

★ Jeans, cords, skirt, shorts, leggings, something else?

　　Color:

　　Fit:

　　Fabric:

　　Condition:

★ Dress, jumper, something else?

　　Color:

　　Fit:

　　Fabric:

　　Condition:

★ Ball cap, painter's cap, beret, fashion hat, something else?

　　Color:

　　Fit:

　　Condition:

★ Jacket—leather, windbreaker, ski, team letter, knit, hooded, something else?

　　Color:

　　Fit:

　　Condition:

★ Shoes—sneakers, running shoes, high-tops, loafers, boots, sandals, or something else? Laced up, buckled or flapping open?

　　Color:

　　Condition:

★ Socks—(color), hose, bare legs?

★ Accessories—earrings, other pierced body parts, necklace, bracelets, watch, belt, something else?

What does the kid look like physically?

★ Hair—color, cut or style? Headband, barrette, scrunchie, something else?

★ Eyes

　　Color:

　　Shape:

★ Glasses—sunglasses or prescription?

★ Lips—thin, generous?

★ Teeth—white gap-toothed?

　　Braces?

★ Face condition—pale, tanned, ruddy, acne, freckles?

★ Hands—calloused, soft, pale, tanned?

Bandages on fingers?

Inked notes or phone numbers?

★ Skin overall—tanned, pale, tattoos, pierced?

Beyond the observation

After you finish making notes about kids' appearances, ask yourself what it tells you about them. If a kid wears blue canvas sneakers with worn white rubber toes and dirty white trailing laces, do the shoes look too small or too tight? Maybe the family is poor. Go beyond the surface and brainstorm explanations for that appearance. Maybe the kid's parents got divorced, the parent who won custody remarried, and the new stepparent doesn't want to waste money on the spouse's first kid. Perhaps a parent is in jail and the older siblings are working, trying to support the family, and are skimping on new clothes for themselves. Or maybe the kids all get their own allowance to buy clothes and school lunch, and this kid wanted to save the money for CDs or action figures instead of getting new sneakers.

Pay similar attention to hair. Is the haircut in style, or is it out of date? If the hair is perfectly cut, maybe the parents pay for trips to the stylist. If the hair is long and lanky, maybe the kid just lets it grow—perhaps to get back at his parents or to rebel against them. Make accurate observations, but then ask yourself questions about possible explanations. You'll read more techniques for creating back stories for these characters in chapter 4, but the first step is beginning to think like a kid.

Minds of their own

Middle graders usually haunt fast-food places with their friends, but small children come into family restaurants with their parents. You may have taken your own kids to such a restaurant at one time. You probably ordered them to be on their best behavior and felt mortified when they climbed on the furniture or made too much noise. Don't cringe or feel the need to "parent" the kids you observe, however. Just watch them, and view their actions through the eyes of a child. When they play with food, what might they be thinking? Maybe they're building architectural wonders they can't make at home, because Mom never serves the right stuff. Why do they seem to talk so loudly they're almost shouting? Maybe their parents are talking to each other and only selectively listening to their kids. The children might feel they have to sound loud to be heard.

Turn your mental volume control down and listen to what the children and their parents say, as well as how they say it. Why did Mom say, "Watch out—your hands are dirty," followed immediately by, "And don't wipe your hands on your shirt!"? What could the child have been thinking to wipe her hands on her shirt? Did she think it was a worse crime to have dirty hands in a restaurant than dirty clothes? After all, she might reason that Mom does the wash all the time, because clothes get dirty every day, but they only go to a restaurant as a special treat.

Don't get mad when the kids crowd the aisles and bang into your table or chair. Ask yourself why that kid is already finished and feels compelled to practice leaps, spins and kicks in the aisle. Maybe he wants to be a superhero. Maybe his parents promised to rent the latest Star Wars movie after dinner, and he's already pretending to be a Jedi Knight. He might also want to make sure his parents don't forget their promise! But kids aren't always devious. Much of the time they say exactly what they think, and do just what they want. When you see a youngster building a pyramid out of mashed potatoes, it doesn't have to mean he's a budding Egyptologist. Maybe he just thinks the restaurant mashed potatoes taste yucky but feel even stickier than the best mud. Then the thought of mud makes him think about making mud castles, but his castle doesn't turn out quite the way he planned—which is why you think it looks like a pyramid.

Watch children in action, and look at the world through a child's eyes. Your readers will recognize themselves when the children you observe walk into the pages of your book.

 **Read the Pros**

1. Read *Maniac Magee* by Jerry Spinelli. See how Spinelli's accurate observation of contemporary kids shows the meeting of cultures believably as Maniac's legend is contrasted with the reality of his thoughts and feelings.

2. Characters in a book observe other characters, also. Read *Flip-Flop Girl* by Katherine Paterson, and see how Vinnie observes Lupe and tries to work out what she's thinking before she gets to know the other girl.

3. Sometimes observations turn out to be nothing like the truth. Read *Write On, Rosy!* by Sheila Greenwald. Young author Rosy works hard at observations as an investigative reporter, but the terrible secret she thinks she's found out about her principal owes more to Rosy's imagination than to accurate interpretation of what she's seen. Also read E.L. Konigsburg's *The Dragon in the Ghetto Caper*. As a future famous detective, Andy relies on his keen powers of observation only to find he's seen people from the wrong angle entirely.

TRY IT YOURSELF: BEYOND THE OBSERVATION

1. Look over your notes of small children you've observed in family restaurants. Pick one child. Become that kid. Charge down the aisle after your sister, chasing her and laughing. What are you thinking? Are you going to catch her and pound her, or are you going to tag her and then run away? Are you acting out a chase scene from a television program or a book? Are you the hero? Why did you leave the table? Have you eaten as much as you wanted? Didn't you like the food? Did you want your parents to go somewhere else where you could get tacos or a burger instead of spaghetti? Or do you know your parents will sit there forever, and you can go back and eat some more in a little while?

2. Listen to what the children say—to each other, a parent or the waitress. Write down the conversation in your character journal. Now become one of the kids. Think about what you said. What was in your mind? Write the same conversation, blending in the child's thoughts about being in the restaurant and eating (or not eating) the food. Think about where the family might have been before arriving at the restaurant. Did they go to a movie? Is the kid stuffed full of popcorn?

3. Next time you go to a restaurant, look at your own food. Imagine you were six years old and looking at the same plate. What would you think about it? In the next chapter you'll find out how to create a fictional character for a story based on a situation like this that you've observed or experienced.

TURN REAL CHILDREN INTO CHARACTERS

Transforming Fact Into Fiction

Remembering your own childhood is a great way to capture the emotions you felt as a kid, and observing contemporary children allows you to use realistic situations in your writing that kids will recognize immediately. However, you need to be careful about using real people in your stories exactly as they were in real life. Suppose your son did something really cute and you use it in your next story—you even name the fictional character after him. If it's a magazine story, it may be published in the next eight to eighteen months, but if it's a book the wait may be several years. When it comes out, will your son be proud to see his long-forgotten embarrassment exposed to the reading world? If his friends see the magazine or the book, will they tease him about it mercilessly? In the interests of domestic harmony, it's a good idea not to expose members of your immediate family so blatantly.

The same goes for childhood friends. If you write about a traumatic memory you and your best friend shared, and you write about your best friend, using her name and describing her in detail, she'll recognize herself. Other friends from your childhood will recognize her, too. And she may not like the way you've described her. You may have shown her honestly, but perhaps she wishes she'd acted differently and resents your betraying her inadequacy. Worse, she may remember the incident completely differently than you do and think she did something you don't remember her doing. In that case, she'll probably be angry with you for misrepresenting her. That's the root of many libel cases in adult fiction, though in the world of children's fiction the result is usually unpleasant damage to a good friendship rather than legal complications.

Transforming reality

You can avoid sacrificing a friendship or a child's affection by changing the character you remember, even very slightly. Does your son have curly black hair and gray eyes and play baseball? Give him a different name, straight brown hair, hazel eyes, and let him play soccer in your story. His friends won't recognize him, and he may not remember the incident that struck you so forcefully. For that childhood friend, start by giving her a new name and appearance. Then ask yourself what quality defined your friend's role in this remembered incident. Was it her loyalty? Her feistiness? The way she charged forward? Or her reticence, and the way she held back? Keep this defining personality trait, but change other aspects of her character. If she wore freshly ironed blouses and skirts, let her wear tailored shirts, vests and ironed jeans. In addition to keeping your friends, there are other advantages to making changes like these.

Often writers limit themselves by what actually happened. They write a real incident from memory just as it occurred, and their characters are exactly like the people they knew in real life. Unfortunately, real life doesn't have the shape of plotted fiction. A child at a turning point that will define character may not identify the significance of that moment for years to come, yet in your story you strive to show the character growth you only perceived later, as an adult. Too often, this leads to stilted fiction. Or you can feel so constrained by "the way it was" that you miss interesting turns your plot might have taken, because you just didn't do that in real life.

By stepping a little bit back from the real people you remember, you free yourself to develop them more creatively. And forcing your character to behave exactly the way the real person behaved in the same situation creates nothing more than a straight, photographic image of a real person—only a shell. The idea is to associate actions, speech patterns, reactions, habits, attire and so forth with certain attitudes and personality traits that the reader can recognize. These are pieces of a character's personality puzzle that will shape the final person on the page.

If you're writing about your family and you grew up in Virginia, set your story in Houston or Seattle. Perhaps your friend who was loyal and

TRY IT YOURSELF: TRANSFORM REALITY

1. Choose one memory from your character journal that includes a friend from school. Give that friend a new name. Give that friend some combination of: new hair color, eye color, wardrobe, hobby. Think about one thing you'd like to change about that friend in the context of that incident—perhaps change an action or a statement, add a character (like that little sister) or remove a distracting friend (a third party) from the scene. Freewrite the incident featuring this changed character. If the character begins doing or saying things you don't expect, follow the trail. Don't be critical of these changes.

2. Unless you were an only child, choose one memory from your character journal about one of your siblings. Give your brother or sister a new name. Give that sibling some combination of: new hair color, eye color, wardrobe, hobby. Think about one thing you'd like to change about your brother or sister in the context of that memory. Freewrite this new version of the incident, and don't be surprised at what this new sibling does, says or thinks.

3. Choose one youngster you observed in chapter 3. Give this youngster a name (if you know the child's actual name, come up with a new one). Don't worry about changing the youngster's appearance this time, but change one variable in your observation. For example, if you observed the youngster shoveling snow, let her rake leaves. If you observed him eating burgers and fries with his friends, let him share a pizza with those friends. If she's playing with her mashed potatoes in the restaurant, change the situation to playing with her coleslaw at a church picnic. Freewrite this new scene.

---

feisty, or who was reticent and held back, was an only child. As you're writing your story, you wish she'd had a kid sister for dramatic purposes, to heighten the way she stuck up for someone who was getting picked on or to emphasize the way she turned her back on incidents when someone smaller than herself was picked on. Should you take such a liberty? Will the power of your memory be diminished by tampering with it? Absolutely not! What gives a story based on a real incident its power is using your feelings about that memory to intensify the experience for the reader. Those feelings can usually be developed more powerfully by altering the facts judiciously.

Your goal should be to write the best story you can, that works to express an idea for the reader. And that idea might be better served by creating new details. Retaining your friend's name and all her personality traits will limit you to nothing but the facts, and your fiction will suffer. By retaining the defining personality traits that impacted this incident, but changing everything else about your friend to suit your story line, you'll emerge with a stronger character. And she'll never recognize herself in your prose and have her feelings hurt.

Read the Pros

1. Read *Ann M. Martin: The Story of the Author of the Baby-Sitters Club* by Margot R. Becker, then read any of the Baby-Sitters Club books, especially the early ones that Martin wrote herself. See how Martin used memories of herself and her friends to create some of the Club characters. Does Mary Anne seem a lot like Ann Martin? How do they seem different?

2. Read *Harriet the Spy* by Louise Fitzhugh. Harriet makes notes about the people in her neighborhood and makes decisions about them based on her notes— in effect, she turns them into characters in her mind. How often are her interpretations right? How often do her interpretations create characters who are different than the real people she observes? Are her characters just as interesting and believable as the real people, or even more so?

Fictionalizing yourself

It's one thing to step back from someone you've observed or a friend from the past, but stepping back from yourself is the greatest challenge. You've explored your memories of growing up in your character journal and found several incidents that grab your interest as potential story material (you'll find many more as you continue to write about your memories). What will inspire the best stories are memories of your feelings about certain incidents. Were you proud of what you did? Were you ashamed of yourself? Do you wish you'd done something different? Write about these feelings honestly, even if it means admitting you're embarrassed at what you did back then.

When you started writing in your character journal, you weren't supposed to question why certain memories triggered strong reactions. Now look back at those that did, and think about their significance. Probably they are either unresolved moments in your past (incidents that you wish had worked out happily, but just seemed to end without any satisfactory resolution), disturbing memories (incidents that should have

TRY IT YOURSELF: FICTIONALIZE YOURSELF

1. Look through your character journal. Do you see a memory that resonates because of something happening in your life today or in the lives of children you know today? Write about the echo in time in your journal.

2. If you don't see such an entry in your journal, look back in your life. Is there an event that you wish you had been able to make turn out differently? Does it still haunt you? Do you see any echoes that tie it to something in your life today or something in the lives of your children, grandchildren or students? Write about the way you wished that event had been resolved in your character journal.

3. Now look into that memory for your remembered emotions. Don't let the distance of time minimize your feelings! Instead, use your writing skills to express your delight or misery as vividly as possible as you freewrite in your character journal. Let your feelings loose and let your words get as impassioned as you can.

---

worked out one way, but worked out a completely different and distressing way) or moments that seem surprisingly relevant to your life today. One of the most interesting things about history is the way it repeats itself. A situation you were unable to deal with when you were ten or eleven keeps cropping up in new guises until you find a way to deal with it at forty or fifty. Or sometimes an unfinished memory from your childhood finds its echo in something that happens to other kids in your adult present—either to your own children or to other children in the news.

Resolving your memories

When you find events from your childhood in your diary or journal that resonate with feelings you're experiencing today or with contemporary events, use your own remembered emotions to help you shape a character who will find herself in a similar situation. She will struggle with the same confusion, fear or pain, but will ultimately be able to deal with it. Often these memories resonate because something similar has happened to you recently in your adult life. For instance, when my family moved to New York City when I was a kid, I found myself isolated from the cliques there who had been together since preschool. I poured the pain of being picked on as an outsider into my diary.

When I moved to a small town in Indiana as the wife of a military officer, I found we were again isolated. Instead of school cliques this time, it was local townspeople who resented the military because of the appropriation of local farmland for the military base. As I struggled to fit into this small town, I remembered how helpless I had felt as a youngster. I wrote in my character journal about the pain of the notes the other kids passed, their cruel teasing, the way they ignored me in school, treating me as if I were invisible. As a youngster, I desperately wanted to do something to make the other kids accept me, but I never actually solved my problems. I just survived until my parents moved a few years later. That lack of completion stayed with me, and when we moved to Indiana, I felt its echo in time. I used these feelings to create Kevin, the main character in *The Proving Ground*. Kevin's father is a military officer who is assigned to a base in a small Midwest town. When they get there, Kevin discovers that the kids at his school hate him because he's military, and he struggles to find a way to fit in and change their minds about him.

In real life, I'd always wondered why the kids were so hostile, but I couldn't figure it out as a kid or see how to change it. When I encountered the hostile townspeople as an adult, I no longer felt so helpless. I did research on the history of the land appropriation that created the base, called a Proving Ground, and discovered that the government had appropriated the farmland over the owners' objections. The government then failed to pay the farmers even though their families were turned off their land on schedule so the Proving Ground could be built to support World War II. These people were forced to live on the charity of friends and family until they were paid. And those same families still lived in the town.

I could understand the community's hostility, and I could also understand the resentment that many people feel when a stranger enters a closed community. I felt ready to write about characters in this situation. But I didn't go back and write about my experiences in New York—I wrote about the town and its problem with the military. I created Kevin and gave him the same desire to fit in that I felt. I gave him the same disbelief and then stunned shock at the way the kids in school treated him. And I found it easier to deal with these strong feelings through the person of another character than I would have if I were writing a story about my real circumstances.

Read the Pros

1. Read *Little Women* by Louisa May Alcott. Then read any biography of Alcott and see how she used memories from her own childhood to create Jo and the March family.

2. Read *The Pigman* by Paul Zindel. Then read Zindel's autobiography, *The Pigman and Me,* and see how he discovered his own pigman. Think about the real experiences he and Jennifer had with their pigman, and how he used them to inspire John and Lorraine and their special friendship with Mr. Pignati.

Transforming yourself

Once you've captured the emotion of the memory, take a deep breath and step back from the reality of the incident and from the child you were then. Writing fiction is completely different from writing your memoirs. Using your experiences in fiction is a way to show your readers the deeper truth of what memory has taught you. You're taking a reality that you only perceived in part while it was happening, and you are recasting it in the balanced world of fiction, where unfinished pains and unthanked kindnesses can find resolution. Do this by letting yourself make changes in what actually happened, while holding on to the reality of your emotions. Just as you did with your baseball-playing son and with the memories of your best friend, make some changes in yourself.

Clearly, I was a girl when we moved to New York, yet Kevin in my story is a boy. That was a major change! The military setting and the dangerous confrontation I could see building in the town as I planned a fictional story based on the incident seemed to work best for a boy as the main character. As soon as I stepped away from my own gender, I felt free to make a number of changes in reality to strengthen the story. For example, the kids I remembered called me names that would seem dated to readers today. By transforming myself into Kevin, I was able to come up with new names the town kids would call him that would work for contemporary readers. I changed the remembered activities I'd wanted to share and was excluded from into school clubs that Kevin wants to join but is frozen out of. But I didn't change my memories of how I felt when I heard those names or when I was cold-shouldered out of the group.

If I'd tried writing too closely about myself in the situation I remembered, I might have felt limited by the fact that I didn't ever successfully deal with the problem at the time, which would have made an unsatisfactory book. Episodes in real life can be unresolved, but your fiction should build to a climax that allows your main character to come to terms with the event still haunting your memory. The core of my memory had to do with finding a way to break the pattern of an outsider breaching the walls of an insider community. Although I

TRY IT YOURSELF: TRANSFORM YOURSELF

1. Look back at one of the memories you singled out in your character journal, and think about ways you could empower a fictional character in that situation to act as you did not. Make notes in your journal about ways you could transform yourself in that memory into fiction.

2. Look at your observations about a contemporary child. Think about what he or she might have been feeling at that moment. Freewrite those feelings in your journal. It can help if you write these in the first person, as if you were that child at that moment. (If you have trouble with this, look at the character interview questionnaire at the end of this chapter.) Freewrite for ten minutes, letting the feelings guide you. Now stop and read what you've written. What might be troubling that child? Could you write a story showing how the youngster grows as a result of dealing with those worries?

---

hadn't done it as a youngster, I'd identified the pattern and learned to break it as I grew up.

When you use a memory like this in your own writing, look for a way to empower your main character to act as you did not. Let your character grow to the point where he can resolve the incident within the framework of your story and discover something about himself as a person. In the book, I let Kevin deal with his move by building the hostility between the community and the military to a dramatic peak in an unexpected attack on the deserted Proving Ground. The attack forces Kevin to finally stand up for himself and for those he cares about. As a result of facing down my remembered demons in the guise of a character's demons in the story, Kevin is free to grow as a character, and readers can grow as a result of sharing his experience.

Warts and all

Just because you're changing some details of your memory or your observations doesn't mean you should polish the characters to the point of perfection—especially if the main character comes from yourself! Some writers feel the urge to smooth out the rough edges and make their main character perfect. But kids know that real kids aren't perfect. They have flaws, as well as strengths. En route to growing into a person who can do the right thing, they do things they wish they hadn't. Even nice kids think mean thoughts. You know this from your own dark thoughts. Don't suppress them. Use them to make your characters honest and believable. In putting characters you've observed, or characters you've lived, into a difficult situation, give yourself permission to let them do or think the wrong things before they find their way to the right thing.

Try to balance your character's strengths and weaknesses. If your character is physically strong, willing to stand up for smaller kids getting picked on and brave enough to be a leader instead of a follower, give her a secret she hides for fear it's a weakness. Your heroic character might believe in dragons, for instance. Or she might have a pet she believes speaks to her. Carry this to an extreme. An antagonist in your story might have a redeeming trait—the simplest example would be a school bully who is abused at home and picks on other kids, until he identifies another kid who's also being abused and suddenly becomes that kid's defender. You could develop this idea by taking a handicapped character who should be sympathetic, and making her hostile and difficult to befriend because of her disability. Or you could take a lazy character and show his struggle to earn money for a new bike without working. In the end, he works so hard to scam other characters out of their money that the reader can see it would have been less work to get a job in the first place! By setting up a certain personality for your character and giving him or her certain traits that surprise the reader, you make the character more believable than a character with overwhelming strengths or overwhelming weaknesses could ever be.

 Read the Pros

1. Read *Mine for Keeps* by Jean Little, then read Little's autobiography, *Little by Little*, particularly chapters 28 and 29. She's very open about her disabilities and her feelings about them in her autobiography. See how she uses these to craft characters in her books.

Character building blocks

Writing from your memories allows you to go back into the past and explore what you felt at the time. It enables you to gently show readers conclusions that might have taken you years to arrive at. One of the great strengths of using a real event in your writing is the ability to look back with an adult's perception and see how you grew as a result of that experience. Then you can enable the character in the story to grow in the same way, so the reader can start down that path herself. You can also take real kids you've observed, get inside of them and develop them into fictional characters to see how you could use their experiences to create pivotal moments for them in a fictional story.

Memory, observation and getting inside of your characters will allow you to transform reality into believable kids in realistic situations. But do you have a story yet? You will begin to take these character building blocks and construct a story from them in Part II.

Character Interview Questionnaire

Interview a fictional character based on one of your journal entries or on one of your observations. Write down the character's answers in a first-person voice in your character journal, as if he or she were chatting with you. And don't answer the way you think a kid ought to answer—answer the questions the way your character really feels.

1. What's your name?
2. How old are you?
3. What are you up to today?
4. Are you having a good time or not?
5. What's in your backpack? School stuff or personal stuff?
6. What's in your pockets?
7. Show me your room. Describe it. Does one of your parents clean it for you, or is it your responsibility?
8. What's in your desk drawers?
9. What's in your dresser drawers?
10. What's in your closet?
11. Look harder—what's on those top shelves in your closet?
12. What's on the floor of your closet, in the far back corner?
13. What's under your bed?
14. What tapes or CDs do you have?
15. Which one do you like best?
16. Do your parents tell you to turn your music down, or do they think it's OK?
17. What's on your bookshelf?
18. Did your parents pick the books there, or do you buy your own?
19. Do you have any books you don't tell your parents about?
20. What's your best hiding place?
21. Has anybody ever found it?
22. What do you keep hidden there?
23. Does your best friend know about your hiding place?

24. Who's your best friend?
25. What do you like best about this kid?
26. How do you two get along? Do you ever fight?
27. What was the last thing you fought about?
28. Are you in the middle of a fight right now? What's it about?
29. Who's the kid you like least?
30. Is he or she in your class at school, on your team or a neighbor?
31. Why does this kid bug you?
32. What would you like to do about it?
33. Do you have any brothers or sisters?
34. How do you feel about them?
35. Are you really close to one of them? Which one? Why?
36. Does that one give you good advice when you need it?
37. Have you ever followed that advice and gotten into trouble?
38. Does one of your brothers or sisters pick on you?
39. What would you like to do about it?
40. Do you wish you were an only child?
41. If you are an only child, do you wish you had brothers and sisters?
42. How do you get along with your parents?
43. What's your mom like?
44. What's your dad like?
45. If you don't live with both of your parents, what happened?
46. How do you feel about that?
47. Would you like to trade your parents for one of your friends' parents?
48. Do you get to spend time with your grandparents?
49. What are each of them like? How do you get along with them?
50. If you haven't met your grandparents, do you pretend sometimes you see them all the time? What are your pretend grandparents like?
51. What else do you pretend?
52. Let's set up some pretend situations. Suppose you were walking home from school all by yourself, and you found a wallet. There was nothing in it except some photos and an ID. What would you do with it? Why?
53. Suppose you found a watch with an inscription on the back. What would you do with that? Why?
54. Suppose you found a mountain bike lying by a deserted stretch of beach one day—no chain, no ID of any sort. What would you do with that? Why?

55. Suppose you saw a bike dropped near a river that was rising. Would you stop and pull it higher, take it away or leave it where it was? Why?

56. Suppose you saw a turtle in the road while your mom was driving you to a game. Would you make your mom stop the car so you could go back and move the turtle? What dialogue would ensue? What would happen if you got to the game late?

PART II
Give Those Characters the Story They Need

CHAPTER 5

IS IT A STORY YET?

Character Growth and Plot Development

Strong, believable characters are the heart of a story, but not all of the story. Stories go beyond character studies to show youngsters at a significant moment, growing and changing because they have struggled to resolve a conflict or achieve a goal.

Suppose you write about a girl who gets up in the morning, gets dressed, goes to school, comes home, plays a baseball game, does homework, has supper and goes to bed. This sequence of events probably isn't going to grab your reader's wholehearted attention, no matter how believably you show each of those actions and how well developed your character is. Kids want tension when they read—the sort of tension that makes them ask, "What did she do then?" with baited breath.

To achieve this tension in your writing, make things difficult for your character. Complicate her life by giving her something she wants that she can't have, something she needs that she can't get or someone out to make trouble for her. Then show her trying to deal with it. This is where completely developing your character becomes so important. Only when you know your character well enough to know exactly what she would do in a tense situation can you believably show her struggling with story conflict.

Plotting your story

To plot your story, you need to come up with a story problem. You might start with a character you developed based on your observations of real children in chapter 3. Then give that character a problem. Or you might start with a difficult situation you wrote about in one of the memories in your character journal, and then create a character to handle it. Most stories don't start with a character getting out of bed in the morning, but you might develop that earlier idea of an ordinary day into a story by giving the character a problem.

Suppose Erin's worried about her baseball game. She plays second base, and she has a lot of trouble making a double play. But this afternoon her team is in the play-offs, and they've got to win to get to the championship. Erin wants to wear her lucky socks (even though they've got holes in the heels) so she'll be sure to make the play if she gets the chance. But when she opens her sock drawer—no lucky socks! She looks under her bed, on the floor of her closet—everywhere she can think. But she can't find those socks. Heartsick, she opens the hamper, and there are the lucky socks, with all the rest of the dirty laundry. Mom forgot to wash them!

Here we see Erin's problem (no lucky socks) and why it matters to her (her team has to win the play-offs, and she's afraid of not playing well). That sets up a story problem that your reader will care about, because Erin cares about dealing with it. Both Erin and the reader feel the tension. Sustain that by making things difficult for Erin. If it's too easy for her to solve her problem—for instance, if she throws her lucky socks in the wash and has time to wait through the washing cycle and the dryer—your story will be over too easily, and the reader will wonder why she bothered reading it. Instead, introduce obstacles to make it harder for Erin to deal with her problem.

Perhaps Erin slept late, and the school bus will be there in fifteen minutes—no time for washers and dryers! What could she do to overcome this obstacle? Perhaps she knows they've got washers and dryers at the school gym, and she decides to take her socks with her to wash there.

What could go wrong? You might show how awful the socks smell and how the kids on the bus make fun of her. What could she do? Maybe she crams her socks in her lunch box, knowing she'll have to throw her lunch away, but willing to do it to play well in the game. Or maybe she hangs her lucky socks out the window so they won't smell and worries all the way that she'll drop one.

Once she gets to school, Erin runs to the gym and puts her socks in the wash. She plans to go back at lunch and throw them in the dryer.

TRY IT YOURSELF: PLOTTING YOUR STORY

1. Brainstorm a list of possible problems that a kid living in a big city might experience. Now pick a different location—a small town, a rural community, an isolated town in the middle of Wyoming, an island—and brainstorm a new list of problems. Think about the ways setting can impact a character's growth as he deals with a problem.

2. Brainstorm a list of possible problems a kid might have in any setting, such as not understanding fractions, dealing with a sibling who's ill and needs extra attention or failing gym because he's afraid of getting his glasses broken. Choose one problem from your list, and create a character to deal with it. A student who's bright in every subject except math might be ashamed when he can't understand fractions, while an art student might not care one way or the other about fractions—until the test.

3. Take a sports-related problem, such as Erin's worries about fielding that double play in her ball game.
   - ★ Write about a gung-ho sports player facing that problem.
   - ★ Now write about a mediocre sports player facing the same problem.
   - ★ Now write about a kid who hates sports facing the problem.
   - ★ What other different types of character can you come up with? How would each of them deal with the problem?

What could go wrong? Perhaps the teacher needs to talk to her, and Erin barely has time for lunch, let alone running to the gym and starting the dryer. All afternoon she thinks about playing in wet socks. What else could go wrong? When she finally gets there, even more bad news—no sign of her lucky socks!

Climax and resolution

Your story plot should build through a series of escalating obstacles. Each time your main character is confronted by another obstacle, she should struggle to overcome it, building to the climax—the worst obstacle of all. At the climax, make it look as if your character can't possibly overcome the last obstacle and is going to fail in resolving her problem or achieving her goal. Erin's story problem is finding a way to wear her lucky socks because her goal is to play well in the game. If she has no lucky socks, she believes she'll be a failure.

Once you back your character into a corner at the climax, it's tempting to help her. For example, it might seem like a fun twist to have Mom rush in just before the game. She felt guilty about not washing Erin's lucky socks, so she looked for them in the hamper. When she didn't find them, she figured out what Erin had done and hurried to school. She and the gym teacher checked the washers and found the socks, and Erin's mom took them home to wash (and maybe even darned those holes). Erin wears the socks gratefully and makes a double play that wins the

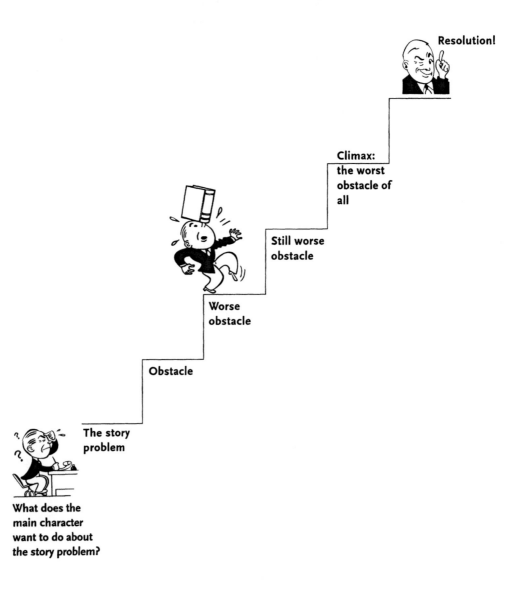

Resolution!

Climax:
the worst
obstacle of
all

Still worse
obstacle

Worse
obstacle

Obstacle

The story
problem

What does the
main character
want to do about
the story problem?

game, with Mom cheering for her in the stands. What's wrong with this ending?

While mothers might love it, kids would feel cheated. They want to see the story character resolve the problem by her own efforts, not be rescued by someone else. In real life, the cavalry rarely sweeps in to the rescue, so having it happen in a story makes the story unbelievable. Besides, reading about fictional worlds where outsiders can be counted on to step in and solve problems can make a kid's real world seem unsatisfactory, or even create false expectations about real life. More importantly, having an adult save the day prevents the character from facing the problem herself. It's the act of facing the problem and overcoming the worst obstacle that allows the character to change and grow—that significant moment that is the heart of a good story.

Here the climax comes when Erin faces the fact that she has lost her lucky socks. She's never going to be able to wear them in the game. She has two choices: She can either give up and run home and refuse to play, or she can face the problem and overcome it by trying her best to play better than she ever has. Because she's not relying on luck, she makes herself think about her playing—and she plays better than she's ever played before! Erin may not make the game-winning play (that's a little pat), but her teammates admire her for her good playing, and she realizes she's an important part of the team and actually has been all along. She has grown as a character because of dealing with this problem, and your reader has grown as she shared Erin's experiences.

Use this same method to plot your fiction, letting the characters you create grow and change believably. You may know what the problem is before you begin, or you may brainstorm a story problem. Then make it difficult for your character to resolve that problem. At the climax, put your character in the worst possible position, where it looks as if there's no way to avoid failure—the character is forced to make a difficult decision. Allow her to dig deep within herself and find the inner strength to make the right decision to deal with the situation.

Read the Pros

1. Read *The Giver* by Lois Lowry. Although it seems as if the Giver has planned a way to return the memories to the community, the situation worsens and Jonas must change the plan and come up with a solution to save himself and Gabriel.

2. Read *The Witch of Blackbird Pond* by Elizabeth George Speare. Orphaned and sent to live with stern Puritan relatives, Kit takes the initiative in befriending

a Quaker woman who is known as a witch. See how the author develops the conflict so that Kit must face the respected adults in the community to defend herself from the suspicion of witchcraft.

3. Read *Bless the Beasts and the Children* by Glendon Swarthout. See how Cotton rallies a group of misfit campers who are criticized by their parents and mocked by the adults who run the camp. As the situation at camp worsens, the boys band together against the adults to free a herd of buffalo before the animals are scheduled to be shot.

Characters want things

Believable characters, just like real kids, want things. Erin wants to play well in the game. Seeing how she reacts to obstacles to get what she wants will develop her personality for the reader. For example, if Erin is frilly, she might agonize that the gym washing machine doesn't have a delicate cycle for her pink socks. If Erin never helps in the house and has outdoor chores instead, she may not even know how to use the washing machine and may have to make numerous tries to get the machine to start. Knowing your character helps you decide how she'll try to get what she wants.

In planning your story, you can either start with a character and then work out your plot details, or start with a plot situation and then create a character to deal with it. If you start with character and then work out the plot, your character's actions, ethics, opinions, personality and what he says (and also leaves unsaid) will help you decide what he wants in terms of a story goal.

★ Shy Greg might want to make friends—or there might be a deeper reason that he's shy. Perhaps it's because his parents fight all the time and put him down. Greg must gain a better sense of his self-worth by dealing with his parents' criticisms before he can make friends. A story about Greg might involve him trying to help another kid. Succeeding helps him realize that his parents are wrong. He *is* important and deserves to be treated differently, so he tells someone he needs help.

★ Bright, outspoken Vito, whose mother has remarried, finds himself in a similar abusive situation. He also has a goal of wanting help, but he'll go about achieving it differently, demanding help before the situation gets out of hand. Or perhaps Vito knows that his mother believes in keeping problems in the family, so he doesn't want to tell someone at school or church. He might hitchhike to tell a favorite aunt and uncle, try to call his grandparents or hold out until his older sister comes back from college at spring break. Or Vito might decide that his mother's opinions are suspect since she married this man. He might talk to a nonfamily member instead.

Sometimes the character you've developed seems pretty happy-go-lucky, with no apparent difficulties in his life. To brainstorm a story, ask yourself what your character wants. These may be simple things you can discover by brainstorming universal desires. Perhaps he wants to make the team, find a friend, get a pet or learn a new skill. Brainstorm a list of desires, and then look at the other personality characteristics you've given this character, or the characteristics you've observed, if you're starting from a real youngster. Choose a desire that seems right for that character. For example, if you've observed a little girl in a restaurant wearing a velvet dress, stockings, patent leather shoes and perfectly tied hair ribbons, you might give her the desire to sing a solo in her church choir instead of playing soccer. But if the same little girl seems restless, her stockings are wrinkled, her patent leather shoes are scuffed and her hair ribbons are tangled—maybe soccer is exactly what she'd like to do! Once you decide what your character wants, come up with a reason why he can't have it. Whatever goal or desire you give your character and how he struggles to achieve it will shape the story that follows.

 **Read the Pros**

1. Read *The Believers* by Rebecca Jones. See how the author begins with her character wanting something: Tibby wants her famous television reporter mother to spend more time with her. When she meets Verl and Esther, whose parents belong to a fundamentalist religious sect, Tibby decides to pray for a miracle—though the answer to her prayer doesn't solve her real problem.
2. Read *Running Out of Time* by Margaret Peterson Haddix. Jessie is content in the 1840 village of Clifton, Indiana—until children come down with diphtheria. Then Jessie discovers that she and her family and friends really live in 1996, and the 1840 Clifton is actually a tourist site. But no one is allowed to leave. To get modern medicine to save her friends, Jessie must escape into a 1990s society she has never known.
3. Read *The Bridge to Terabithia* by Katherine Paterson. In the beginning, Jess simply wants to be the fastest runner in fifth grade. But when Leslie moves next door she first proves to run faster than Jess can and then opens his eyes to worlds of imagination that only they can share. When tragedy strikes, Jess must confront an entirely different problem in learning to live without his friend.

TRY IT YOURSELF: WHAT CHARACTERS WANT

1. Select a character you've written about in your character journal. List six things this character would like to be in the short term, such as the team captain or the star of the drama department play. Next to each item on the list, briefly explain why the character wants that and why it will be hard for her to become what she dreams.

2. Use the same character or select a different character you explored in your character journal. List six things this character would like to have, such as a puppy, a big brother or new sneakers. Next to each item on the list, briefly explain why he wants it and why it might be difficult to get, such as your character having allergies or not having enough money to buy a puppy.

3. Use the same character or select a different character you wrote about or observed in your character journal. List six things this character would like to do, such as make straight As, go to Disneyland or get tickets to a Cowboys football game. Next to each desire, briefly explain why it's important and why it will be hard to get.

Characters have problems

A character may have a fundamental desire that shapes his story, or he may be surprised by the story problem. Something unexpected goes wrong in his seemingly perfect world, and he has to deal with it. His parents could decide to move, for example. Kids feel at home in the community where they grew up, and moving can be a great shock. Sometimes the story problem is deliberately caused by someone else—an antagonist who dislikes the main character or wants to hurt him in some way. This could be a kid at school who has it in for your protagonist—a school yard bully is the first example that comes to mind. It could also be a kid who wants to get the best grades and is upset because the protagonist starts getting higher science grades, or a kid who's determined to be class president and makes trouble for the protagonist because she senses a possible rival.

After you come up with a problem that matters deeply to your character, and decide what he wants to do about it, ask yourself what steps he's going to take to achieve this resolution. The answers to these two questions—1) what he wants to do, and 2) the actions he is going to take to try to achieve that goal—probably won't be the same. For example, in *The Proving Ground*, Kevin's problem is that his Army officer father has moved the family into a small town that is hostile to the military. What Kevin wants to do about being moved to a new town is make some friends so he'll fit in. As a character, Kevin is quiet and careful not to make waves and embarrass his father, so he wouldn't do anything flamboyant. The way he tries to make friends is to join a club after school.

After your protagonist makes the first attempt to resolve his problem, you should introduce an obstacle to prevent him from succeeding so early in the story. The other kids throw Kevin out of the club because he's military. Their ringleader is a girl who has a personal reason for hating the military— a girl Kevin likes on sight, very much. What can Kevin do next? He tries to understand why she hates the military. When he does, he finds her and tries to apologize for the way the military appropriated her family's farm to build the local base where his father serves and his family now lives. What can go wrong? Not only does the girl refuse his apology and nearly start a fight with him, her cousin threatens him with violence.

What can Kevin do next? He discovers that the house his family is living in once belonged to the girl's family. Somewhere in the house is a secret hiding place, which Kevin believes holds something that he can give back to the girl. He hopes the return will change her mind about the military. So he stays home one day when everyone else has gone to the town's winter fair, the biggest event of the year. But the tension between townspeople and the military has escalated to the point that local teenagers attack the deserted military base that afternoon—and Kevin is the only one in a position to stop them.

In the beginning, Kevin's goal was simply to make friends and fit in, but by the climax of the book his goal has been transformed into preventing a disaster, regardless of personal consequences. As the situation worsens for your character, what he wants to do about his original problem will evolve. To help him reach that point, present at least three major obstacles, each one making things worse and worse for him. As he attempts to deal with each obstacle, he'll grow and change. That character growth shows the reader ways that he, too, can grow by working through his problems. It also adds depth to your story and your character, as you'll see in the next chapter.

Read the Pros

1. Read *Stolen Bones* by Joan Carris, and see how Alec's attempts to have a good summer in Montana evolve. In the beginning he's looking forward to spending

a summer on a real dinosaur dig with his paleontologist grandfather. But when his grandfather appears to have a grudge against him, Alec tries to solve the mystery of some missing dinosaur bones to change the man's mind.

2. Read *The Voyage of the Frog* by Gary Paulsen, and see how David's goal changes. In the beginning of the book, he tries to cope with his Uncle Owen's death by sailing his sailboat out to scatter his uncle's ashes. When an unexpected storm sweeps over the boat, David finds himself lost at sea, struggling to stay alive.

3. Read *The Alfred Summer* by Jan Slepian. While trying to deal with his cerebral palsy, Lester inadvertently befriends Alfred, who is retarded. As the two of them join forces with two other outcasts to build a getaway boat, Lester stops trying to excuse himself and discovers just how "special" he and his friends really are.

A Plotting Questionnaire

By asking yourself a few questions, you can take a character you've created (or a character based on a child you've observed) and develop a story plot for that character. Use the answers to these questions to help you work through escalating obstacles to climax and resolution.

1. Who's your main character?
2. Boy or girl?
3. How old is he?
4. Where does he live?
5. What's his family like? Does he have two parents, one parent, live with grandparents or foster parents? Does he have brothers or sisters? How many? Are they older or younger?
6. What could go wrong in his life? Or what goal does he want to achieve?
7. What does he want to do about the problem (the long-term solution)?
8. How is he going to try to deal with the situation? What are the incremental steps that he hopes will help him achieve the long-term solution?
9. Who else is involved? If it's a school problem, perhaps his teacher, a best friend or an enemy is involved. Or perhaps it concerns his parents, siblings or neighbors.
10. Of those other people involved, who will help him? How?
11. Of those other people involved, who will make it harder for him to solve his problem? How?
12. What does he do first to deal with the situation?
13. What obstacle could make it harder for him to deal with things? This could be another character getting in his way, an event that compli-

cates things or an inner weakness that makes it hard for him to do what he wants to do.

14. What time frame exists for solving the problem? A deadline adds tension because the character (and the reader) is constantly aware that time is running out.
15. What will he try next to solve his problem?
16. What could go wrong with the solution he attempts?
17. What will he try next?
18. What obstacle will set up the story's climax?
19. What decision will he make or what action will he take to achieve the resolution of his story problem?
20. How will he have changed as a result of dealing with this situation?

TWO PROBLEMS IN ONE

A Character's Internal Problems

Plot resolution is the action that allows your character to solve the story problem. However, strong children's stories succeed on two levels. If the plot action is the only level, editors and readers will find the story superficial. The level beyond this surface action gets to the heart of the significance of character development. What is Erin's story really about? On one level, it's about solving the mystery of her lucky socks and winning the game. On a deeper level, however, her story is about the importance of overcoming superstitions and developing confidence in herself. The decisions the character makes to deal with the story problem also resolve an internal problem that illuminates the change and growth at the heart of your story.

Erin's story problem is playing successfully in her baseball game. That's the external action of the story. Her struggle to wear her lucky socks is really a way to guarantee she'll play well. But Erin has an internal problem as well, one inextricably linked to her external problem. She lacks confidence in her playing skills, so she feels she must rely on the lucky socks to make that double play.

A story climax serves as a moment of truth when your character must dig deeply within herself and see what she is really made of. When Erin realizes the socks are gone for good, she searches within herself to decide whether to go home and give up, or go forward and play anyway.

If she decides to play, she could tell herself that she doesn't stand a chance without her lucky socks, and blow the double play. Or she could rise to the occasion and make up her mind to play as hard as she can. If she does that, she will find herself a changed person after the game: a player who relies on concentration and skill rather than luck.

Believable character growth

Because the reader identifies with your main character and wants to share the character's growth, you need to insure the transformation that occurs at the moment of crisis is believable. Your character may draw on inner qualities she wasn't aware she possessed, but these can't come as a complete surprise to the reader, or the ending will seem coincidental or unconvincing. If Erin's successful fielding results from how much she loves baseball and how hard she works at it, then set this up. Let us know that she's never missed a practice and drills at the plays even after practice lets out. She may lack confidence, but she doesn't lack the drive to work at what she loves, and that practice will pay off when she gives it a chance.

Not every character is capable of rising to the occasion, of course. This is particularly true in books for older readers. A teenage Erin might realize that a player who still relies on lucky socks in her senior year of high school has no talent for the game. She may quit the team to concentrate on a different hobby—but one that she has no talent for, either. In this case, her internal problem would be a refusal to discover where her true talents lie. This could be underscored by having her choose an activity that she also hopes to succeed at by luck. The reader would see the teenager's blindness even if the girl couldn't, and the point would be made. While that type of resolution is honest and rings true for teen readers who have seen that the world has no easy answers, most fiction for younger readers uses positive resolution as a way to help kids mature. Erin's positive growth would offer guidance, rather than a warning.

As readers look ahead to the adults they will become, they are constantly faced with choices and decisions. While parents may tell them what they should do, kids are more influenced by what they see others they admire doing—and by what their favorite story and book characters do. They vicariously experience the story problem along with the main character, and they share his desires and doubts. When that character makes a difficult choice and grows a little as a result, the reader asks himself if he could make the same choice. If he admires the character enough, he may try out the same behavior when he finds himself in a similar situation—and discover the same opportunities for growth in real life.

74

TRY IT YOURSELF: CHARACTER GROWTH

1. Brainstorm ways a small child could grow—becoming more independent, for example. A preschooler might decide to play trucks with the child next door, instead of playing by himself at home. A primary grader might decide to ride the school bus with her friends instead of having Mom drive her. List other ways small children grow and change. For each one, come up with a story incident that might bring about the change.

2. Middle graders change and grow in different ways. They take on more responsibilities. They begin to question what parents say in contrast to what teachers and friends say, and they begin to deal with peer pressure. List specific ways middle-grade characters might change and grow. Next to each way, come up with a story incident that might trigger the change.

3. Making a difficult choice can be an opportunity for character growth, such as deciding whether to wear the sweater Mom likes or a sweatshirt like the other kids wear, especially if the character likes (or dislikes!) them both equally. Brainstorm a list of situations where the character has to choose between various actions or conflicting desires. Make the choices believable rather than simplistic (a cookie or a carrot for a snack) or preachy (buying candy or saving the money for a Mother's Day present). Force the character to look inside himself honestly. Select one of these situations, and write a scene where your character makes one choice and defends it. How does she grow? Now write a scene where the character makes the other choice and defends it. How does she grow differently?

Read the Pros

1. Read *Ella Enchanted* by Gail Carson Levine. Ella's curse requires her to obey each and every order. See how she grows by loving her prince so deeply that she cannot obey him when he asks her to marry him, for fear that the curse could endanger him and his reign. Her refusal breaks the curse.

2. Read *The Lottery Rose* by Irene Hunt. See how Georgie grows by coming to terms with his history of abuse by his mother and her boyfriend. In the beginning he lavishes all the love he wishes he could experience on a rose-

bush he wins in a grocery store lottery. Despite the adults who try to help him, Georgie only grows to trust again when he recognizes someone else who has also been hurt, and he uses his rosebush to heal them both.

3. Read *The Chocolate War* by Robert Cormier as an example of a realistic resolution for older readers. See how Jerry tries to stand against the other kids and teachers by refusing to sell school chocolates. In the end, Jerry decides that he can't win against them, and it's better to give in and do what they say. This lets readers see how a fictional character can fail to rise to the occasion, and it makes readers wonder what they would do in their own lives.

The significance behind your memories

Real people change and grow with life's vicissitudes, and those moments of change and growth stand out in our minds. Look back at the memories you wrote about in your character journal. Chances are they stayed in your mind because you grew a little as a person. Perhaps you changed something about yourself or about the way you saw someone or something outside you as a result of that incident. Beside these entries, make some notes about the changes you remember in yourself.

For example, one writer's memory involved finding an injured fledgling and struggling to help it get well in spite of warnings that wild animals always die in captivity. The incident stayed with the writer because the bird lived and flew away. The child who would grow up to become a writer discovered that faith and love can prevail over common-sense warnings and other people's failures. That gave her confidence to trust herself in future decisions. When the writer wrote a story inspired by that incident, she could let her fictional character grow in the same way. The external action involved the efforts made to save the bird, but the internal problem involved questions of faith and confidence.

An incident can also stay in your memory because you made the wrong choice or missed an opportunity. The same writer remembered wanting to buy a magazine but being too shy to go up to the newsstand alone, even though her parents urged her to. The incident stayed in her memory because she wished she'd been brave enough and always wondered when she would find enough courage inside herself to risk trying something new. In a story based on that memory, Amelia wants to buy a book but is afraid to go shopping. When Amelia finds the courage to approach the tall counter and buy the book, she discovers that shopping isn't so frightening after all. The external problem of the story is the action of going shopping, while the internal problem involves Amelia's shyness and the courage it takes to overcome that shyness so she could go up to a stranger and buy something.

TRY IT YOURSELF: USE YOUR MEMORIES

1. Select a memory in your character journal where you can see how you grew and changed as a result of the event and your decisions and actions in response to it. Create a character in a similar situation who will change in the same way. Write a scene that allows the character to grow and change as you did.

2. Select a memory in your character journal where you made the wrong choice and wish you had done differently. Create a character in a similar situation, but allow that character to make the decisions you wish you had made. Plan a short story in which you could use this character.

3. Select a memory in your character journal that stayed with you because it puzzled you. Perhaps you didn't realize the significance of it at the time and only years later understood its impact upon you. Decide how a youngster might perceive the impact sooner, and create a character who can do so. Use this incident as the basis for a short story.

 **Read the Pros**

1. Read *The Chalk Box Kid* by Clyde Robert Bulla, along with his note at the end about the trouble he had coping with new places as a child. To let Gregory deal with the problem in the story, Bulla gave the boy something he'd always longed to find: a blank wall he could draw on.

2. Read *Lily's Crossing* by Patricia Reilly Giff. Lily's adventures in Rockaway (including the scene in which she and her friend eat the candy meant to be sent as a care package to the friend's brother fighting in Europe) were based on Giff's actual childhood memories of summers at the beach during World War II. In the book, however, Giff gives Lily a friend who adds tension to that summer holiday—Albert, a young Hungarian refugee from Nazism.

Starting with action

Sometimes you will start with the external problem and need to develop an internal problem to show the character growth. This can often happen in a mystery or adventure story, where the action is paramount. However, a story that shows only action without character growth will be superficial. So dig deeper and learn a little more about your character and why he finds himself in the middle of this situation. Suppose Carlos is sitting in a fast-food restaurant, and he looks out the window and sees a classmate walk down the sidewalk—but that kid is supposed to be dead! (Kids love creepy stories, especially middle graders.)

To develop your story, you need to know how Carlos is going to react based on what his relationship with the other kid is (or was). That tension will move your story forward, so Carlos's inner problem will come from some lack or concern related to his feelings about this classmate. At this point, however, all you know is the starting situation. You may also know the answer to the mystery about the "dead" kid. To understand Carlos's character growth, however, ask yourself some questions about Carlos and how well he knew this classmate before the other kid supposedly died.

First decide if the classmate is a boy or a girl. Then ask yourself how well they knew each other. Did they only see each other in school, or were they neighbors? Had they gone to camp together, or were they in the same sports team, or in a club or a church group together? Decide if they'd known each other all their lives, just this year in school or only a few weeks. Now decide whether or not they liked each other and why Carlos liked or disliked the other kid.

If the other kid faked her death and ran away, decide whether or not Carlos knew it—and whether he helped. He might be afraid that he'll get into trouble now that she's back, or he might be worried about what will happen to her. In this case, his inner problem might be a tendency to run away from problems, and he needs to learn to confront them. If they were best friends and he missed her terribly, then he'll feel differently at the sight of her. Perhaps he'll feel eager to talk to her again, but also hurt that she hadn't gotten in touch with him instead of just strolling down the street, not even looking for him. Or maybe the other kid knew a secret about Carlos, and Carlos felt safer with her gone. Now that she's back, he might be afraid that she will tell his secret. Decide what he might be hiding. Would he try to stop her from telling? In this case, his inner growth might come from realizing that secrets should not always be kept.

If the classmate really is a ghost, maybe Carlos witnessed his death. Perhaps they were playing at mountain climbing together on some dangerous rocks, and the other kid fell. Maybe Carlos felt guilty because of the accident, or maybe he didn't tell anyone what happened, and he felt guilty about that. In this case, his inner problem could be coming to terms with his guilt and his responsibility toward his friend. Or maybe

TRY IT YOURSELF:
ACTION AND CHARACTER GROWTH

1. Write a short story in which Carlos looks up and sees his classmate's ghost and reacts, using one set of answers to the questions above. Reveal Carlos's character growth as the story progresses to its climax.

2. Now use a different set of answers to plan a completely different story starting from the same scene. Let Carlos grow and change differently in this story.

3. Start with an idea you have for an action story. Make a list of character traits and skills based on the action. Does your character have to climb a rose trellis at the climax to solve the mystery, for example? Perhaps she should be agile and strong. Or perhaps this is a way she can grow—perhaps she should start out afraid of heights or a real klutz, and have to overcome this to succeed. Based on your list of traits and skills needed for the story action, make a list of the character's qualities and abilities and potential lack of the right qualities or abilities needed to solve the problem. Develop these in the context of a story to show your character's growth.

4. Look at an action story you've been working on that lacks character growth. Ask yourself what point your story makes for young readers—what you want them to take away from reading it. Your character's growth should emphasize that point, so think of a change or realization you could give your character to accomplish this. Try to develop the character's motivation so that his need to solve the problem reflects the growth you want him to experience.

---

the other kid knew something that Carlos thinks he needs to know—a secret about his missing father, for instance, and he will need to confront the ghost to learn the truth. In this case, perhaps Carlos will realize that finding out about other people is less important than finding out about himself.

Once you know the background of their relationship, you'll know how Carlos will react to the sight of his classmate. He might jump up and chase the other kid openly, sneak after her or run into the bathroom and throw up. Perhaps he would sink under the table in shame, or slink home embarrassed. After you know how he reacts, you'll be on the way to developing your plot and Carlos's character growth at the same time.

Character first

Often you will start with a good idea of your character and how you want her to grow and change, but you will lack a plot. Your character's growth might come about because of some quality she lacks. For example, perhaps you want to write a story about a youngster who feels helpless, and you want her to discover that she can make a difference. In that case, think of a situation in which the girl would feel helpless. Perhaps a teacher failed Sara on a test, and she thinks she should have passed, but she never argues with teachers. To learn to stand up for herself, Sara needs a strong motivation to challenge the teacher. Perhaps this isn't just any test—it's the final, and if she fails, she'll fail the class. This makes the need to take action imperative, so Sara must figure out what happened and convince the teacher to give her another test, or persuade the teacher to pass her on the first one. That will generate your external story action, based on the internal problem of learning to overcome feeling helpless.

The danger with using a fundamental character flaw is that your story can get preachy. If Kira's problem is that she's selfish, then your story can degenerate into a morality tale in which Kira learns that it's better to be generous than selfish and reforms her ways ever after. Often in this type of story, the character is caught and punished and learns the lesson. While this is the essence of great tragedy (Hamlet and Macbeth are each destroyed by their character flaws), these stories don't persuade young readers to be less flawed—they merely encourage kids to stay away from preachy stories. If Kira's inner problem is selfishness, find a creative way for her to discover that selfishly keeping everything for herself may leave her without anything that matters in the end.

Instead of a character flaw, you may start with the opposite: Sometimes a character strength can cause a problem. Characters often have special abilities or special knowledge that everyone else makes fun of, sometimes to the point that the character becomes ashamed of these qualities or wants to use them to get revenge on the kids making fun of him. Ryan obsesses about dinosaurs, for example, and the other kids get bored hearing about nothing but paleontology. At the climax of the story, however, Ryan's fascination is exactly what is needed to save the day. Perhaps Ryan's class goes to the natural history museum and some of the kids tease Ryan that he should stay there because that's where he belongs. When they chase him into a deserted display area, one of the kids bumps into a strange device that turns out to be an experimental time machine, and they're all transported to the Triassic period. Only Ryan knows how to survive there. He might be tempted to get his revenge on the other kids, or he might discover the value of working together as a team.

80

TRY IT YOURSELF: CHARACTERS LEAD TO PLOT

1. Select one of the memories a family member shared with you about his or her childhood. Ask yourself what a modern reader could take away from a story based on this memory. Decide how a character's growth in a similar situation could make that point for the reader, and use a combination of the memory and character growth to plot a story.

2. Make a list of tangible things a character might need, such as a new winter coat, a friend, a bicycle, money for a school trip or a pet. Select one item, and think about a character who would need it and why. Perhaps a girl needs a pet because she's lonely and wants something alive to play with. Decide how she'll find a way to get her pet or perhaps to get something else that fills that need. Then plot a story that shows how your character grows as she solves her internal problem.

3. Make a list of intangibles a character might need, such as love, understanding, discipline, guidance or sympathy. Choose one, and think of a concrete situation in which the youngster would need that. For example, a boy whose single mother works long hours might need guidance. Decide how he will fill this need, then plot a story that allows him to grow as he does so.

4. Make a list of places where a kid wouldn't normally find himself, such as in a museum storeroom, at international peace negotiations or backstage at the Metropolitan Opera. Choose one, and decide what sort of kid might find himself there and what plot developments might have gotten him there. How would his personality and background help or hinder him in that situation? How would he grow from being thrown into that unusual setting? And how can you tell his story most effectively? In the next chapter, you'll find out how to choose the best voice for your story.

Whether you start with the external problem or the internal problem, you can weave the two together to create a strong character who resolves both. Your readers will discover something about themselves as your character grows and changes in your story.

Read the Pros

1. Read *The Fox Maiden* by Elsa Marston. The author started out by creating a character who wanted to have a new experience and to prove herself by entering an alien world and living there successfully. But Marston also made her headstrong, ignoring warnings that what she wanted to do could be dangerous. See how her determination, ambition, courage, curiosity and overconfidence work to bring her to the book's climax.

2. Read *The Reluctant God* by Pamela F. Service. The author started with a plot situation: An ancient Egyptian teen would be magically mummified and revived in modern times, but would only speak ancient Egyptian. Service needed to create a modern kid who could speak with him and help him. Raised by an Egyptologist father, Lorna uses ancient Egyptian to ridicule other students at her hated boarding school. She's a self-reliant loner who has experience doing things that will help her work with the awakened mummy to recover his treasure, such as managing an international flight. See how she possesses the abilities needed to cope with the plot.

3. Read *Hot Fudge Pickles* and its sequel, *Marshmallow Pickles*, by Marilyn D. Anderson. In the first book, Anderson started with plot. She wanted to write about a kid who convinced a whole town that pickles dipped in hot fudge sauce tasted good. She imagined an eleven- or twelve-year-old redheaded con man who would convince his friends that hot fudge pickles were tasty and could even make adults go along with the idea, including the mayor. The book took off as Alvin Jones grew more and more real. In the sequel, Anderson started with character, knowing Alvin already and asking herself how she could put him in a position where he could make the biggest mess involving pickles.

CHAPTER

WHO'S TELLING THE STORY?

Point of View

Once you've created your character and plotted a story to show that character's growth and change, you're ready to start writing. But how will you introduce this protagonist and his situation? Kids identify with a story's main character as they read, so they want to get inside that character's heart and mind right away. To help them do this, write the story from the point of view of the character you've created. Become your main character as you write. You know him well, so you should be able to think his thoughts and feel his emotions, and express them naturally on the page.

Writing the story from your character's point of view means looking through his eyes at the other characters, setting and action as it unfolds. In real life, you may sometimes guess what someone else is thinking, based on her expression, her actions and how well you know her, but you're not really sure. Your viewpoint character is in the same situation: He knows what he's thinking and feeling, but he can only observe other characters. He may know some of them well enough to guess what they *might* be thinking, but he won't be sure about others. It's tempting to write:

Andy sighed. He didn't know the answer. Who cared what day President Lincoln was assassinated? It was over and done with!

What mattered was figuring out how he was going to deal with Sherri after school.

Mr. Williams frowned at Andy. Didn't the boy ever do his homework? What were parents thinking, sending their children to school unprepared? Things were very different when he was growing up. "Your answer," he prodded.

Sherri grinned. She knew Andy hadn't read that history chapter last night. She'd caught him in her backyard, digging for worms. If he didn't pay up after school, she'd tell on him— out after dark, and trespassing too! He'd pay, all right.

Kids reading this story will wonder which character to care about. Is Andy the main character, or is Sherri? And they probably won't care what the teacher thinks about his students not doing their homework. To draw the reader into the world of your story and the mind of your main character, you need to write the story consistently from that character's viewpoint. For example, you could take that scene and write it from Andy's point of view:

Andy sighed. He didn't know the answer. Who cared what day President Lincoln was assassinated? It was over and done with! What mattered was figuring out how he was going to deal with Sherri after school.

He saw Mr. Williams frowning. Why did the teacher make such a big deal over homework? If it mattered, he ought to teach it in class, not expect kids to waste their own time reading history.

The teacher prodded, "Your answer."

As Andy wondered what to say, Sherri caught his eye and grinned. Andy couldn't believe she'd caught him in her backyard last night, digging for worms. If Dad found out Andy was outside past his curfew and in someone else's yard, he'd ground him for sure. No fishing for weeks! But how could he pay what Sherri asked?

Now it's clear that Andy is the viewpoint character. The reader shares his thoughts and feelings, and sees Mr. Williams and Sherri through Andy's eyes, without ever losing track of Andy himself. The voice also sounds natural for a kid, so the reader feels at home in the story. For example, one could write:

As Andy pondered his response, he caught a glimpse of Sherri grinning at him. It was incomprehensible how he had allowed himself to be caught the previous night, seeking fresh bait on her property.

The reader wouldn't believe this paragraph at all. That's clearly an adult voice, and it distances the kid reading the story from the action and the character.

My very own story: First-person POV

Establishing your protagonist as the viewpoint character in your story is one thing. Now you need to decide whether to write the story in the first person ("I did it"), the second person ("you did it") or third person ("he did it"). The first person makes the story immediate for the reader:

I wondered what I could say so Mr. Williams would leave me alone. Then I caught Sherri's grin—and forgot all about class-work again. How did I let myself get caught? And by Sherri! Why didn't I go over to Aaron's and dig in his yard? Sherri's going to get me grounded for life, or at least until all the best fish are already caught. But I can't pay what she asked, can I?

Andy becomes more personal. Not only can the reader identify with him in the story, but as he reads it can almost seem as if he has become Andy.

The first-person voice is flexible. Instead of just writing the story in a standard narrative form, as previously, the narrator might be speaking directly to the reader, as a friend:

I wondered what to answer. You know those cats who play with mice, smacking them around between their paws? That's Mr. Williams, all right. You know what I mean. You've had a teacher like him. So you'll understand when I say he was the last thing I needed when I was busting my brain trying to figure out what to do about Sherri before she ruined my life.

The narrator might be writing in a diary. This style is particularly popular in historical fiction, but it can also be used in a contemporary story. Or the narrator might be writing E-mails to a friend:

85

To: Marco@spur.com

From: Fisherking@inet.com

Man, I'm glad you're around—you've got to tell me what to do. Sherri—the freak—caught me! Her yard is just perfect for digging, and I had these great worms, and then I looked up and there she was! Now she's going to tell Dad unless I pay up!!!! On top of that, Williams the sadist was all over me in history class.

This type of narration can be very effective, but should only be used for a purpose. Unless the computer E-mail connection is significant to the plot development, it will seem an artificial device well before the end of the book.

The first person allows your character's true voice to shine through, but it can be challenging because you have to make sure that every word is exactly what your character would think or say. You must keep your adult voice in the back of your mind as you write, and concentrate solely on the kid who's telling your story. But the effort can be a reasonable price to pay to achieve the immediacy of the first person that plunges the reader into your story.

Liar, liar

Some first-person narrators can't tell the truth, any more than some real kids can tell the truth. An unreliable first-person narrator will seem totally convincing, so that the reader accepts everything the narrator says—at first. As the story develops and the facts don't add up, the reader will become suspicious of the narrator and will finally come to see the truth. These unreliable narrators can add tension to a story, particularly for adolescent readers. Perhaps Andy is a deliberate liar, intending to mislead the reader. He might tell the reader what happened when Sherri saw him digging for worms, but leave out the fact that he wasn't supposed to be out after dark, and make it sound as if Sherri was going to make his actions appear much worse than they were just so she could blackmail him.

Or Andy might be lying to himself unconsciously when he lies to the reader—he can't tell the reader exactly what happened because he refuses to accept the real truth. Maybe Andy has convinced himself that his parents didn't want him to go outside after dark, but it's OK to be in the backyard because they really meant that he couldn't go to a friend's house. Then he further rationalized that Sherri's backyard was right next to his, so he wasn't really away from his backyard. Anyway, he certainly wasn't at a friend's house, so he wasn't really violating curfew, but Sherri could make it sound as if he were and get him in a lot of trouble he doesn't deserve. This attitude will impact the way Andy thinks about the situation and will change the way you as a writer present it to the reader in Andy's first-person voice. In a story like that, character growth might come from the character realizing how important it is to see the situation for what it really is, instead of lying to himself and others.

Sometimes a narrator can be deceived. He believes he's telling the truth when he relays information to the reader, but the information he was given was false. For example, suppose Andy had just moved into the neighborhood. Where he came from, everybody had a fence, so he knew just where his backyard ended and the neighbor's yard began. But here nobody has fences. Suppose he was digging for worms after supper, right at sunset. He doesn't think he's out too late, and he thinks he's in his own backyard—and he's right. But Sherri wants to take advantage of him. She tells him he's crossed the line and is actually in her backyard. And she tells him that his parents will be even more mad because it's actually dark and he should be inside, but she won't tell if he pays her. In this case, Andy would believe her, and think he's telling the reader the truth about his trespassing, when he's actually not.

Sometimes the action itself will contrast with the first-person narrator's account of things. Suppose the story starts with Andy digging in the backyard, feeling delighted to find some great worms for fishing. But the next day in class he thinks virtuously that he was only in the yard, hunting around for his favorite pen that fell out out of his window while he was doing his homework, and came across the worms by accident. After reading both accounts, the reader will become suspicious about Andy's veracity. Sometimes a different character will come to appear more trustworthy as the story develops, and the reader will begin to look to that character for corroboration before believing the narrator. Sometimes the narrator will discover that he has been mislead, and his narration will become more reliable as he questions where truth lies. Or he may face the fact that he has been lying to himself or to others and come to terms with the necessity of being honest with the reader.

And some narrators never admit the truth, forcing the reader to decide for himself what to believe. This technique can often force older readers to evaluate their own assumptions in light of first accepting the narrator's story, and then realizing it's a false perception of what really happened.

TRY IT YOURSELF: FIRST-PERSON POV

1. Look at the plot you developed about Carlos seeing the ghost in chapter 6. Using the first person, write the scene in which he first looks up and sees the classmate. Become Carlos and think his thoughts. Write the scene as if he were telling the reader about it, friend to friend.
2. Write the same scene in Carlos's first-person voice as if he were writing in a journal.
3. Write the same scene in Carlos's first-person voice as if he were writing an E-mail to a friend who doesn't know what originally happened with the classmate.
4. Write the same scene in Carlos's first-person voice, as if he were telling the reader about it, but this time make Carlos an unreliable narrator. Decide what he doesn't realize himself or doesn't want the reader to know about the situation, and write a convincing scene in which he only tells the reader what he wants him to know.
5. Take one of the short stories you wrote based on a memory in chapter 6. Rewrite it in the first person, from the point of view of the main character.

Read the Pros

1. A strong first-person voice is true to the age as well as the personality of the reader. Read *Alexander and the Terrible, Horrible, No Good, Very Bad Day* by Judith Viorst, and see how Alexander's narrative voice rings true for a primary grader facing an endless barrage of catastrophes.
2. Sometimes the narrator writes a diary, and the entries allow the story to unfold for the reader. Contrast the way Avi does this in *The True Confessions of Charlotte Doyle* with Charlotte's journal, and the way Joan Blos does it in *A Gathering of Days* with Catherine's diary. In *Letters From Rifka*, Karen Hesse achieves a similar effect by having Rifka write letters to her cousin as she flees Russian anti-Semitism with her family.
3. Read *Dancing on the Edge* by Han Nolan. Miracle appears to be giving the reader an accurate account of her life, but see how it becomes clear as the story unfolds that she is an unreliable narrator.

The challenge of *you:* Second-person POV

Very few stories are written in the second-person voice, because readers find it difficult to believe in "you" as the main character. In this voice, you would write:

> You sighed. You didn't know the answer. Who cared what day President Lincoln was assassinated? It was over and done with! What mattered was figuring out how you were going to deal with Sherri after school.

It's hard for a reader to believe in that voice, although a strong writer might well pull off an experimental story in the second person. This can be an effective voice for poetry, but in prose it sounds contrived, and distances the reader from the story action and characters, rather than drawing him into the world of the story.

In reading the first-person examples where Andy addresses the reader or writes an E-mail to his friend, you'll see that he uses "you" quite a lot. That's different from writing in the second person, however. The "person" designation in voice refers to the main character. If the main character is "you," then the voice is second person. If the main character is "I" and is speaking or writing to someone referred to as "you," then the voice is first person.

One genre where the second person works successfully is the "Choose Your Own Adventure" books. Here the reader imagines himself the main character, and the story evolves through the reader's choices:

> You're in the backyard digging for worms. You look up to see a girl glaring at you.
>
> "You're in my backyard!" she says. "You're going to be in so much trouble!"
>
> If you tell her it's your backyard and to beat it, turn to page 7. If you tell her you're sorry and ask her not to tell on you, turn to page 8. If you throw a worm at her and run for home, turn to page 9.

The second-person voice can work very well in situations when you want to address the reader directly. Sometimes writers do this in participatory stories for very small children. For example, you would address the reader directly in a hidden objects book where the child searched for an apple for the teacher in a busy classroom, then turned the page and was asked to search for a banana in a scene with monkeys and trees:

See the monkeys play. One monkey isn't playing. That monkey is eating something good. Can you find the banana in the picture?

If you were writing a story where you wanted the reader to sing a song with the characters, you might also use the second person to invite the child to participate:

Darren goes fishing with his grandmother. They sing "Row, Row, Row Your Boat" as they paddle to the best fishing spot. Would you like to sing with Darren and his grandmother?

On the next page you might have all the words of the song to help the reader sing along.

Nonfiction frequently uses the second person to speak directly to the reader. Much of this book is written in the second person, addressing you as you read it. Craft articles or recipes for children use the second-person imperative to tell the reader what to do. When you write, "Thread the beads on the string" you're implying the second person "you" in the instructions. Nonfiction also uses the second person to involve small children in an article by asking questions:

Look out the window. It's snowing! Do you know that every snowflake is special? No two snowflakes look alike! Do you know why?

The child cares more about remembering the answers because the questions seem aimed at her personally.

For older readers, the second person can make an informational article's subject more relevant:

You push a small plastic box across a rubber pad, press on a button with one finger, and your computer suddenly launches a new program or opens a document. How did that little box do that? And why is it called a mouse? When personal computers were first invented, the mouse didn't exist—users had to type commands on the keyboard.

You can also use the second person to show the reader why she wants to read a self-help or a how-to article, by letting her realize that she shares the problem the article addresses. For a piece that offers baby-sitting tips, for example, you might write:

You duck as your charge throws her teddy bear at you. Her parents only left five minutes ago, and now she's screaming that she hates you. How did you get yourself into this mess? Don't worry—you're not the only kid who's ever found himself in a tough sitting situation. Here are some tips for calming down your charge—and yourself.

Although you probably won't use the second-person voice to illuminate character very often in your writing, keep it in reserve as a useful voice to involve your reader in your nonfiction, and an experimental voice to use with fiction. Sometimes trying to write a scene in the second person can free you up if you're having trouble getting into your writing. Later, you can always rewrite that section in the first- or third-person voice.

Read the Pros

1. Read *If You Give a Mouse a Cookie* by Laura Joffe Numeroff. See how the author uses the second person to involve the reader in this humorous tale of actions and consequences.
2. Read "The Hobbyist" by Chris Lynch in *Ultimate Sports*, edited by Donald R. Gallo. See how the author uses the second person to pull the reader into the desperation of a kid who's hopeless at playing sports, yet longs to be part of the game.

TRY IT YOURSELF: SECOND-PERSON POV

1. Experiment with the second person by writing the scene in which Carlos sees the ghost in that voice. Remember that you would be writing it as if the reader were the one seeing the ghost.
2. Look through your character journal and select a small child you observed. Use that child as the basis for a "you" participatory story that involves the reader in an activity such as playing a game or singing a song.
3. Try writing a short how-to article in which you tell the reader what to do and how to do it.

He did, she did: Third-person POV

Most stories are written in the third person. Here you refer to the character by name and by the third-person pronouns, "he" or "she." For example, here is the third-person version of Andy's story:

> Andy sighed. He didn't know the answer. Who cared what day President Lincoln was assassinated? It was over and done with! What mattered was figuring out how he was going to deal with Sherri after school.
>
> He saw Mr. Williams frowning. Why did the teacher make such a big deal over homework? If it mattered, he ought to teach it in class, not expect kids to waste their time reading history.
>
> The teacher prodded, "Your answer."
>
> As Andy wondered what to say, Sherri caught his eye and grinned. Andy couldn't believe she'd caught him in her backyard last night, digging for worms. If his dad found out he was outside past his curfew and in someone else's yard, he'd ground him for sure. No fishing for weeks! But how could he pay what she'd asked?

In this third-person version, the writer remains anchored in Andy's viewpoint, showing the reader only what Andy feels and perceives about the characters around him and his situation. This allows you to express your character's emotions, and show his sense of humor (if he has one) and his attitude toward other characters. It also lets the reader share his confusion or his confidence. But the third-person voice differs from the first-person narrator, who deliberately chooses to tell his story to the reader, or write about it in a diary or to a friend.

The third-person voice allows the writer to skip the deliberate intention of the first-person voice. When a reader reads a first-person story, he can't help but notice the narrator's presence as more than just the main character, and he's got to wonder why the narrator is sharing this experience. Often the writer will come up with a device, such as having the narrator write a diary so the world will know the truth, or as an assignment for school, or because he's in a juvenile detention center and his shrink has asked him to write it. Sometimes the writer will have the narrator explain why he's telling his story. For example, Andy might preface his story by saying:

> Everybody knows about the great fishing escapade in the summer of 2000—or everybody thinks they do. But I'm writing this

down to prove that you don't know the half of it. This is the real truth of what happened. I swear.

But no explanation is needed for the third person. It's a quick, easy way to get the reader into the story and into the character's head. Kids usually read for the sake of the story, and they want to jump right into it. A first-person narrative voice can be very effective, but it can also distract the reader from immediate emotional involvement in the story. The reader knows, after all, that he's not the one experiencing the narrator's feelings, even as he wants to suspend disbelief and allow himself to identify with the main character. He may be more cautious about entering into the world of a first-person story.

Third person can also be easier for beginning writers. In the third person, the vocabulary and syntax should sound natural for the main character in terms of his age and personality, but you don't actually have to write in the character's inner voice the way you do in the first person. You must still remain anchored in the main character's head, however. This means that you, as the writer, can't step outside of the action to let the reader know what's going on in someone else's head or someplace other than where your character is. A reader will be confused if you write:

> Andy's flashlight showed him three fat worms wriggling around in the hole he had just dug. Grinning, he picked them up, one by one, and added them to the collection in his can. He was thinking about going fishing the next afternoon. President Lincoln's assassination was the farthest thing from his mind.
>
> But on Walnut Avenue, across town, Mr. Williams, Andy's teacher, was thinking about President Lincoln. As he planned his lesson for the next day, he wondered whether Andy would know the answer for the change. He was a nice kid, but he never paid attention in class.
>
> Sherri was paying attention, but not to her homework. She was paying attention to Andy, who wasn't digging worms in his yard at all. He was digging in hers. It was a wonderful opportunity.

When done correctly, however, third person is the least obtrusive writing style, so the reader will pay more attention to the story and the characters than to the writing style.

TRY IT YOURSELF: THIRD-PERSON POV

1. Look back at your answers to the questions about Carlos and his ghost. Using a different set of answers than you did when you wrote the scene in the first person, write a new scene in the third person. How does it differ in tone and style, beyond the plot differences necessitated by the new answers?

2. Take a character you wrote about in chapter 5 who wanted something. Write a scene in which he can't have what he wants. First write it in the third person, and then write it in the first person. Which version do you think shows the scene more effectively?

3. Select one of the scenarios you plotted at the end of chapter 6 to show character growth. Write a story in the third person that shows your character resolving both her internal and external problem.

 Read the Pros

1. Read *Awake and Dreaming* by Kit Pearson. Note the way the author writes Theo's thoughts and feelings in the third person, but draws the reader completely into her world.

2. Read *Nobody's Daughter* by Susan Beth Pfeffer. See how Pfeffer makes it clear that Emily is the main character immediately. By the time Emily's emotions deepen at the story's climax in chapters 10, 11 and 12, however, the intensity of the third-person voice allows the reader to completely share Emily's anger, helplessness and determination.

3. Read *Face to Face* by Marion Dane Bauer. See how Bauer uses a strong third-person voice to establish Michael, her main character, as an unreliable narrator, and how this voice allows the reader to experience Michael's struggle to find a father's guidance and his own courage.

When everybody's opinion counts: Multiple POV

While it's important to stay anchored in your main character's point of view in writing for younger children, books for middle graders and above frequently benefit from switching back and forth between viewpoints. There's not usually room to do this in a short story, but a novel's length allows you to develop characters other than your main character more completely. Using this technique, you would focus on two or three significant characters in the story. One of them might be the viewpoint character in the first chapter, and then you would switch to someone different as the viewpoint character in the next chapter. You might write all the chapters in the first person, each in the unique voice of that particular character; you might write all the chapters in the third person; or you might write one character's chapters in the first person and another's in the third.

However, you must have a reason to use this technique, beyond just wanting to get inside of different characters' heads for your own pleasure. Switching viewpoints should enhance the story for readers in some way. If your first-person narrator is unreliable, for example, then chapters that let readers see into the mind of a different character could help them decide who's telling the truth. Perhaps one character knows something another significant character doesn't realize, and the reader must know both sides to understand what's about to happen. In some books, multiple viewpoints enhance the theme. Perhaps none of the viewpoint characters fully understand what has happened, but the reader comes to see a larger picture by sharing each character's perspective, and grows through the experience of putting the pieces together for himself.

Using multiple viewpoints can be risky, however. Unless it's done extremely well, readers can be confused as to which character they should care most about and identify with. They may feel distanced from the story to the point where they don't care about any of the viewpoint characters, which simply makes them put the book down and go to something else more satisfying. Avoid this technique in writing for younger readers. Let them focus on one single character and get caught up in the story action with that character.

When using this technique for older readers, take the time to introduce each viewpoint character and develop him or her before shifting to the next one, so the reader can get to know each in turn. Also make it clear when you're switching viewpoints. You might do this by using each narrator's name in the chapter heading, as Virginia Ewer Wolff does in *Bat 6*, or you might clarify this for the reader in the very beginning of each chapter. For example, you could establish Andy's point of view by writing:

Andy sighed. He didn't know the answer. Who cared what day President Lincoln was assassinated? It was over and done with! What mattered was figuring out how he was going to deal with Sherri after school.

TRY IT YOURSELF: MULTIPLE POV

1. Think about what might happen in the rest of Andy's and Sherri's story. Write one scene from Andy's viewpoint, then write the next scene from Sherri's viewpoint.
2. Try a new take on the story about Carlos and his ghost. Take the scene you've written about Carlos first sighting the ghost, and write a scene that follows it from the ghost's viewpoint.
3. Look back at the list of problems you brainstormed in chapter 5 based on dealing with a setting. Write a scene from the perspective of a character new to one of those geographical locations. Then write the next scene from a character who's lived there all his life.

When the next chapter begins, you could establish Sherri as the viewpoint character by writing:

Sherri watched Andy fumbling around in class and grinned. She knew he couldn't figure out how she'd caught him in her backyard or why she was blackmailing him about it. That was fine with her—let him stew a while. She had plans for him.

When you use multiple viewpoints, you sacrifice the immediacy of strong identification with one character, but you gain an advantage of being able to shift from one location to another, as well as from one character's mind to another. Some stories simply can't be told unless the reader knows what's happening in two different places simultaneously. But you should use this narrative voice judiciously, and take the time to fully develop each character. If you do so, you can end up with a rich, complex novel that will be worth the effort readers invest in it.

Read the Pros

1. Read *Being of Two Minds* by Pamela F. Service. See how the chapters alternate between Connie's thoughts and Rudy's thoughts once the author develops each of them as well-rounded characters with their own problems—one of which they share in common. Here both viewpoints are written in the third-person voice to make it easy for the reader to concentrate on the story action when Rudy is kidnapped and Connie must try to rescue him.

2. Read *Nothing but the Truth* by Avi. Although it's clear that Philip is the main character, the story unfolds though a series of Philip's diary entries, school memos, news clips, statements, personal letters and conversations by the other characters involved in the confrontation between a rigid but fair teacher and a frustrated student who unintentionally breaks a rule.

3. Read *The Pigman* by Paul Zindel. See how the chapters alternate between John's and Lorraine's first-person voices, speaking consciously to the reader as they promise to tell the whole sad, yet wild and wonderful, story of their friendship with Mr. Pignati.

Standing back from the action: Omniscient POV

Occasionally writers find that the best way to tell their story is to stand outside of it, literally telling the reader what happened rather than letting the story unfold through the perspective of any one character. Fairy tales are an excellent example of this omniscient point of view:

> Once upon a time there was a handsome prince, an enchanted princess and a wicked queen.

The writer is inviting the reader to settle back and be told a story, but not to enter into it. This technique allows the writer to dip into everybody's mind at will:

> The handsome prince longed to prove himself when he rode out of the palace. He thought he was seeking a dragon, but little did he know that he was about to discover just how a true prince might prove his nobility and wisdom.
>
> Meanwhile, the enchanted princess worked hard for the wicked queen. She knew something was missing from her life as she scrubbed all the goblets and platters from the feast the queen had enjoyed the night before. Because of her enchantment, however, she didn't know what it might be. That it might be a handsome prince come to rescue her never crossed her mind.
>
> But the wicked queen (who had laid the enchantment on the princess in the first place) knew exactly what would break the spell and free the maiden, so she was on the lookout for any handsome prince who might try to ride across her drawbridge.
>
> "Ladies only!" she would cry. "Begone!"
>
> And every prince would apologize, bow deeply and ride away. Until this prince, that is.

The reader is carried along with the story, often enjoying the fact that he knows more of what's going on than any character in the story does. In the guise of the omniscient narrator, the writer can offer asides to the reader, commenting on the action or the characters. Stylized stories such as fables and fairy tales benefit from this technique, and many picture books are written in the omniscient voice. Writers assume that an adult or an older child will read a picture book to the smaller child, and the story-telling omniscient voice works well when read aloud.

This technique is less effective for older readers, except in the hands of a strong writer who deliberately uses a fable to make the reader laugh or stand back from the follies of the characters to see them more clearly. If you want to write a realistic, true-to-life story, choose the first person, third person or multiple viewpoints rather than the omniscient voice. But if you're writing a fairy tale, fable or picture book, consider experimenting with an omniscient voice.

Base your final choice of which narrative voice to use for your story on the advantages and disadvantages of each option. Ask yourself whether the first person's own natural voice will add to the story or distract the reader from it, or if shifting viewpoints will increase the tension or the mystery, or detract from it. The form you choose for your story should flow from the story and its characters. It's all right to experiment with writing part of your story in several different voices before choosing the one that feels right to you—the one that will carry the reader into your character's world.

 Read the Pros

1. Read *Holes* by Louis Sachar. See how the author steps back from a third-person voice that focuses on Stanley to an omniscient voice that tells the reader the history of Green Lake and the story of Stanley's "no-good-dirty-rotten-pig-stealing-great-great-grandfather." He lets this fable for older readers develop back and forth between the omniscient voice and the third-person voice.

2. Read *Gwinna* by Barbara Helen Berger. See how the omniscient voice enhances this fairy tale for older readers.

3. Read *Through the Mickle Woods* by Valiska Gregory. See how the author uses the omniscient voice in this picture book to show both Michael and the king as they struggle with grief. The author further enhances the power of her tale by allowing the wise bear to tell them three stories that help them heal their pain.

TRY IT YOURSELF: OMNISCIENT POV

1. Take the story of Carlos and his ghost, and experiment with writing it in the omniscient voice. What do you lose in standing outside of the characters? What do you gain?

2. Write an original fairy tale in the omniscient voice, as if you were telling the story to a listening audience. How effective is this when written down, as opposed to spoken aloud?

SHORT CHARACTERIZATION FOR SHORT STORIES?
Short Fiction

Good character development and growth can take hundreds of words to explore fully. But most magazine stories for middle graders only run 800 to 1,200 words, while those aimed at younger children only run about 500 words. Short stories in anthologies may only run between 1,000 and 3,000 words. Having spent hours developing your character and your plot, it's difficult to condense both into so little space. Successful short stories still require strong characters, but you need to focus on specific qualities rather than showing every aspect of your character.

Significant background

A short story leads your character to a resolution that is a significant turning point in his life. A book, however, covers a sequence of moments of growth in response to the character's conflict that build to a climax of profound revelation and change. Given the space constraints of a short story, you must introduce the story conflict immediately. Then develop your story by showing the reader only what he needs to know about your character to get the character to that turning point.

Story characters, like real people, carry a lot of baggage—they have memories, personality quirks and preferences for which type of ice cream they like best and what television programs they watch. While you need

Main character is confronted by story problem.

Obstacle to main story problem arises.

Main character overcomes first obstacle only to be faced by subsequent, and worse, obstacles.

Story climax: The main character overcomes the worst obstacle of all to resolve the original story problem.

Main character is confronted by initial problem.

Obstacle to initial problem arises.

Problems relating to character's friends intrude.

Problems relating to character's family life intrude.

Problems relating to character's job or school life intrude.

Unexpected problems from other characters and circumstances intrude.

These problems should either:
★ relate to the novel's main theme
★ complicate the initial
★ enhance character growth

Main Character struggles to deal with the initial problem as increasingly worse obstacles arise.

At the story climax, the main character overcomes the worst obstacle of all. This might resolve one of the additional complicating problems, rather than the original main story problem.

to know your character in detail to understand her personality, you won't need all of those details in your story. For example, when you plan your camp story, you decide that Keesha's problem is that she's a city girl in a camp situation. Keesha knows all about:

* riding subways
* going to museums
* going to heavy metal concerts with friends
* singing along with her CDs and MTV
* avoiding muggers
* swimming in chlorinated pools
* bargain shopping for cool clothes.

But Keesha doesn't know anything about:

* surviving in the camp wilderness
* riding horses
* watching out for snakes
* coping with smelly latrines
* shaking spiders out of her shoes
* cooking outdoors.

At this point, you know a great deal about Keesha—what sorts of clothes she likes to wear, what heavy metal groups she likes best and what songs she sings, whether she prefers the art museum or the natural history museum and why, how she avoids muggers, whether she swims for fun or is on the swimming team, and why she's going to camp in the first place (probably because her parents talked her into it—or maybe because she was going to go with a friend, but her friend backed out). Pick and choose among all this material to decide what's going to be significant for your story. Her swimming will be important if they swim at camp—but perhaps they swim in a pond with a muddy bottom instead of a chlorinated pool. This might be a significant detail that has the potential of either adding to her troubles in camp (she hates the muddy pond), or helping her deal with the problem (she impresses the other campers with her swimming skills and makes some friends). Her museum escapades, subway experience, bargain shopping, interest in MTV and prowess at avoiding muggers will probably be less important to your story, and the reader may not need to know about these qualities at all.

TRY IT YOURSELF: SHORT-STORY CHARACTERS, PART I

1. Choose one character you've developed from your memories in your character journal. As you plot a short story, certain character traits, memories and personality quirks you know from your own experiences will be significant in the way this character will deal with the story problem. Decide which other qualities you can discard because the character doesn't need them for this story situation.

2. Choose one youngster you observed in chapter 3 and developed further in your character journal. What you see from the outside can be different from what you know about a character you've generated from your own memories. As you plot a short story, decide which of the character traits, memories and personality quirks you've already given this youngster will be significant, and which ones you can discard for the purposes of the story plot.

As you plan out your plot, decide which details are significant. What memories does Keesha have? How will they impact her experience at camp? The idea of not wanting to be there is a good starting point, but you need to know a little more about the plot development and how you want Keesha to grow as a person to know what details you should give the reader about her. You might want this story to show her overcoming a terrible fear and discovering that she has to admit this fear instead of keeping it secret before she can overcome it. What could that fear be? In the context of a camp story, it will have to relate to something she might encounter at camp. Perhaps there was a fire in the apartment building where she lived when she was little, and Keesha has always remembered her terror at the smoke and the flames. At camp, there will be cookouts and campfires, and Keesha has never come to terms with her terror at the remembered fire.

She has other memories—of learning to ride a bike or getting a perfect attendance award in Sunday school—but these memories are not significant to the story you're writing. She probably has other fears as well. Maybe she's afraid when the power goes out in the city; maybe she's afraid of dogs. But those fears won't be important for this particular story. Once you focus the character growth in your mind, you will be able to select significant details that make your character real in the world of your story.

 **Read the Pros**

1. Read *But That's Another Story . . .* edited by Sandy Asher. See how each author in this anthology gives the reader just enough information about their characters to allow the reader to become acquainted with them in the context of each story.
2. Read *Join In*, edited by Donald R. Gallo. See how each author focuses on plot-specific characterization to show kids in various ethnic communities in the United States.
3. Read short stories in *Cricket* and in *Highlights for Children* magazines. See how the authors develop their characters using details and personality traits that are significant for the plot and character growth.

Target your audience

In addition to keeping your characterization short and tight for short stories in magazines and anthologies, you also need to suit the degree of characterization to the age of the character—and the age of the reader you're targeting. Kids like to read about someone who's about their own age or a little older, so keep this in mind when you decide which age group to target. This applies to all of your writing for children, of course—novels as well as short stories. Keesha, with a complex internal problem that includes both her fear and her determination to keep it a secret, would appeal most to older, middle-grade readers. Younger children would have trouble dealing with the different levels of her problem. And Keesha's activities and interests are in keeping with what middle graders are doing.

A camp story for younger readers might still focus on a way the main character feels afraid of the different surroundings, but the fear and the character's growth would be simpler. For example, a younger Keesha might love the horses but be afraid of bugs, so she's scared of the horse-flies. She runs and hides or thinks of other excuses when her tent group is supposed to go for their riding lesson. All that the reader might need to know about this small Keesha would be that she's scared of bugs, likes animals and has never been to camp before. Where she lives (her city background) wouldn't be as important, and other considerations like her swimming experience could be ignored. If swimming is a camp activity that happens in the story, Keesha could simply be learning along with the other campers.

Your characters should never be flat, but you want the degree of characterization to be appropriate to the age group you're writing for. Middle graders find out a great deal about their friends. They collect facts about them the way they collect baseball cards and series books. Younger children accept a playmate on the basis of far less information—one or two quirky traits will make these kids come alive. Readers relate to the characters they befriend in the same way.

Conflict complexity

The intensity of the character's internal and external problems in both short stories and novels varies based on the age group you're targeting as well. A mystery for older readers might involve Nate's teacher accusing him of cheating, when he knows he didn't do it. To solve the mystery he might have to bicycle from one place to another and interview school friends or other teachers. The story could even end with him hiding out in the classroom closet, trying to trap the culprit. A mystery for younger readers would be simpler—perhaps Timmy hunts for a missing toy truck. He could search for clues in his backyard, talking to his sister or his father or his dog. He might find the missing dump truck in the flower bed or in the sandbox. The settings are closer to home, which small children will find familiar. They could imagine themselves solving a mystery at home. The setting can cover a wider range and the problem can increase in complexity for older readers, who venture farther afield in their own lives.

In addition to making the action less complex for younger readers, the internal problem the character faces should be less complex as well. Both mysteries could revolve around the internal problem of responsibility. Nate's internal problem is one of honor. He knows he didn't cheat, but no one believes him, and he must prove himself responsible enough to have done the schoolwork himself, or everyone will consider him a cheater. Perhaps he has backed down in the past when he was accused of something less important, taking the easy way of least resistance by just letting people think he did it, even if he didn't. In proving what really happened, Nate's confidence in standing up for himself when he knows he's right will increase. But that's way too complicated a situation for a small child.

Timmy might deal with responsibility on a much simpler level. Maybe he always gets into trouble with his parents and older siblings because he loses all his toys, but he's been trying to be really careful about taking care of them. He knows he was playing with his toy truck in the yard, but it's not with the other toys he was playing with. In

1. Pick a middle grader from your character journal. Give the character a goal and a story problem. Select three or four character traits that will be useful in dealing with the story problem and offer room for character growth. Write a 900-word short story about this character.

2. Pick a young child from your character journal. Give him a goal or a problem, and select one or two character traits. Then plot a simple story where the child deals with the situation and discovers something about himself in the space of 500 words.

3. After reading some rebuses for small children, plan a 100-word picture story with simple action. Choose only one fact and one quality about your character—she wants to play ball and she can't catch, for example, but she's spunky. If you use too much information, you'll run more than 100 words, so keep her characterization tight and focused as she finds a way to achieve her goal.

---

remembering what he did all day and exploring the yard with his dog, Timmy might notice his dog dragging things around and hiding them. When he finds his truck covered with sandy dog drool, he realizes that the dog was the culprit, and he's right that he's becoming responsible enough to look after his own toys. In each instance, the character changes and grows, but this development reflects believable growth in a child of that age, and does it within the length restrictions of a short story.

Read the Pros

1. Read the short fiction in *Cricket* magazine, geared to ages nine to fourteen. Contrast the character depth and growth with the fiction in *Spider* magazine, for younger readers who still read independently. Now contrast both with the fiction in *Ladybug* magazine for smaller children whose parents read to them. All three magazines are published by the Cricket Group and are subject to the same editorial requirements, but the characterization in the stories differs considerably, based on the age of the targeted readers.

2. *Highlights for Children* contains magazine fiction for all ages in one publication, from read-aloud stories for the smallest children through rebuses (picture stories) and up to read-alone stories for older kids. See how the background

information the reader gets about the characters varies based on the readers' ages.

3. Read the short fiction in *Turtle* magazine. Contrast the character depth and growth with the fiction in *Children's Playmate Magazine*, which is targeted to slightly older readers. Now contrast both with the fiction in *Children's Digest* magazine for readers up to thirteen. All three magazines are published by the Children's Better Health Institute, and manuscripts are evaluated for all of the CBHI's publications. See how the story characters for older readers have more depth and grow in more complex ways than the characters in the read-aloud stories for smaller children.

Picture books

Like magazine short stories, picture books must develop in only a short space. But a magazine story may be read once, while a successful picture book will be read again and again. What invites the reader to do this is the immediate connection your character makes with the reader. This means that your characters must be strong and appealing and work both for the preschoolers who will listen to the book and for the adults who read the book aloud. The character's attempts to resolve the story problem should be visual, either taking place in a number of different settings or involving lots of vivid action, to support illustrations on every page.

You don't need to know as much about the background of your picture-book characters as you need to know when you write a longer book for older readers. Picture books tend to deal with universals that help the reader instantly identify with the character, whether you're writing about a child, animal, vegetable or creature from the realms of fantasy. The story situation may involve being reassured that parents will always be there even as the child grows older, making or keeping friends, proving that a child is more grown-up than parents or siblings realize or discovering the magic of a summer day or a winter snowfall. The reader brings his own senses to the story and accepts the character at face value.

What the reader wants to see in a picture book character is potency. If your story shows how Eleanor tries to fill a boring, rainy afternoon when the power goes out and there's no television, then you must introduce her frustration and determination to do something about it in the very first sentence. If you first spend time describing the rainy day or start with Eleanor's happy morning before the rain starts and the power goes off, the reader's enthusiasm will wane. The illustrations show the setting—your story itself should jump right into the action and emphasize the character's response to the situation.

Character growth in a picture book will not be as profound as in a story for older readers. Eleanor will not have the resources of an adolescent character to sneak out of the house, go to the mall with a friend and discover that sometimes it's better to explore the possibilities in your own home than insist on finding external diversions. However, the resolution should show her drawing on inner resources that the reader can recognize and identify with. In the course of her rainy afternoon, perhaps Eleanor fills the house with exciting friends from her imagination, and turns each room into a different adventure—a safari among the stuffed animals in her bedroom, for instance, and a tea party with the Queen of England in the kitchen.

When the storm passes and the power comes back on, Eleanor is more interested in continuing to explore her imagination than in switching on the tube. Perhaps she even turns off the lights, so she can go back to exploring the shadowy cave under the dining room table. Eleanor establishes her potency by dealing with the situation in a way that grows out of her character. To focus this you would concentrate on the universals of her personality: her boredom, her determination to do something about it and her vivid imagination. Other character information, such as her favorite kinds of candy and whether she sits quietly in church, have no place here and would only distract the reader from the power of her story.

 Read the Pros

1. Read *The Rat and the Tiger* by Keiko Kasza. See how the author focuses on the universal concept of making friendship work by playing fair and allowing both characters to work out how to be equal.

2. Read *Very Boring Alligator* by Jean Gralley. See how the author establishes the story problem immediately, and then allows her character to discover the importance of standing up for oneself and telling people (or alligators) exactly what one means.

3. Read *Where the Wild Things Are* by Maurice Sendak. We know very little about Max, beyond the fact that he's a wild mischief-maker. See how easy it is to share his fun with the wild monsters.

Real people

Remember that the kids who read your stories may react to your characters differently than you expected. The characters you create are real to your readers, and a character that one reader likes and believes in will impress another reader as being unlikable or even uninteresting. Readers may hate a character, just the way some of your friends will dislike one person you like. There's nothing wrong with this, because the reader is responding to the character as she would respond to a real person. Your characters may be focused tightly for short stories or may grow in deeper and more complex ways in books, as you'll see in the next chapter. Either way, there's no higher praise for your characters than to have real kids meet them in your writing and like or dislike them on their own merits.

COMPLICATE YOUR CHARACTER'S LIFE
Book-Length Character Development

The effort you've put into working out the subtle details of characterization comes into full play when you realize you've got a story to tell that requires a book to do it justice. While a chapter book could run up to 10,000 words, a novel for middle graders may run 25,000 to 30,000 words. Greater space means you can give the reader more depth of character and complexity of plot development. You still shouldn't exhaust the reader with every detail you've worked out in your character biography of your protagonist, antagonist and secondary characters, however. Use significant details that will illuminate your character more deeply, and let incremental stages of character development show the character's progress toward the main growth and change that will come at the book's climax.

Background information

To write a novel, you really do need to know everything about your character—or you will need to discover everything about your character as the writing proceeds. But some details will always remain private, between you and your character. Often writers who plan a lengthy and specific character biography (based on your Character Questionnaire from chapter 4) want to share each and every fact with the reader. That's not the purpose of a complete biography. The purpose is to allow the writer to know instinctively what the character will do at every plot twist and turn. Writers often say their characters surprise them. Sometimes that's because the character has been so fully drawn in the writer's mind that he has taken on a life of his own. For example, you know that Carter watches old Star Trek reruns on TV. But you're writing an outdoor adventure so he never watches television in the book. This fact seems irrelevant. At some critical moment, however—say, when he walks into a murky cave he's sure no one has ever explored—he may intone, "To boldly go where no man has gone before" to give himself courage. If you didn't know that was his favorite TV show, you wouldn't think of that quote as you wrote the scene. He might just straighten his back to make himself feel braver, and then walk into the cave. The action is enough to hint at his attempt to give himself courage, but doesn't say as much about him as the quote from his favorite show implies.

If you know that this is Carter's favorite show, then you also know why. Perhaps he imagines himself to be cool and logical, like Mr. Spock, or brave, daring and humorous like Captain Kirk, or clever at solving mechanical problems like Scotty. This will spill over into the way Carter acts when he's trying to live up to his image of his hero. Other background details work in the same way. You know that Kelly eats Wheaties for breakfast, but if we never see her eating Wheaties in the context of the book, that's fine. That detail about her can still impact on her behavior. If she eats that cereal because it's the breakfast of champions and she's determined to be a champion swimmer, her drive will shine through in all she does—or tries to do. Her preference will be significant without your awkwardly manufacturing a scene in which Kelly grabs her Wheaties, or tells another character what she eats for breakfast.

Sometimes knowing something unspoken about a character helps you build tension. Perhaps your character is so afraid of facing the truth that he has suppressed a certain memory, but flashes of it surface in his dreams. The reader sees glimpses of those dreams, but doesn't know for sure what happened until it either slowly comes into focus through enough pieces of the puzzle, or the character faces the memory and reveals it at the end.

In *Counterfeit Son*, I have Cameron strain to remember something about his abusive father, something the man told him. But he can't quite hear the words in his mind, although many of his father's threats and orders run through his memory, constantly hammering at him even though his father is dead. The mystery surrounding Cameron hinges on what his father told him, and he only slowly drags it into conscious

TRY IT YOURSELF: BACKGROUND INFORMATION

1. Select one of the character sketches in your character journal. Choose one personality trait or preference you gave the character, such as a tendency to keep a messy room, or a favorite book or movie. Ask the character why. Write a short monologue in which the character explains this or justifies it.

2. Look at a character problem you've developed in your journal. Think of a secret the character has or a memory the character has suppressed that could intensify the problem. Develop this in a new plot outline.

---

memory at the very end. However, it influences every action he takes and every decision he makes throughout the book.

 Read the Pros

1. Read *Face to Face* by Marion Dane Bauer. See how Michael can't remember exactly what happened on the last afternoon he spent with his father before his parents' divorce. That suppressed memory, however, has defined his life since, resulting in his inability to deal with school bullies, his stepfather and his own fears and courage.

What's at stake?

In a short story the character faces a fairly straightforward problem. Nate, from chapter 8, would make about three attempts to prove he didn't cheat, facing obstacles that weaken his confidence in convincing his teacher, before he hides in the classroom closet, waiting for the real cheater to sneak into the room after school. In a novel, the stakes would be higher so his motivation would be greater. If Nate's problem is demonstrating to others that he didn't do what he was accused of and proving to himself that he can stand up for himself, the incident of cheating might be only one aspect of this problem.

Perhaps he also knows that other kids believe he's been stealing school supplies because his family is poor. Nate has pretended to ignore these suspicions because he wasn't sure who the real thief might be (though perhaps he had an idea), and he had no way to prove his innocence. But now suspicions are stacking up, and the problem has become imperative, as there's something Nate can't get or can't do while he's under suspicion. Perhaps he goes to a private school on a scholarship, and the accusation of cheating is the last straw that may get him thrown out of school. That gives him a strong motivation to break his habit of backing down and not defending himself.

As he struggles to prove his innocence, other problems stack up that increase the pressure on him. In a short story, the plot development is more linear: The character's problem worsens through obstacles to a climax that is the resolution of that initial problem. But a novel is more sweeping, like life. The character may be confronted with one main problem at the beginning, but as the plot develops things become messier. Additional problems crop up that are more difficult to deal with. Unlike real life, however, these problems should relate to the book's theme in some way. Dealing with a secondary problem may give the character insights needed to solve the original problem. On top of the cheating and stealing accusations, maybe Nate has family trouble. His kid brother is being teased because Nate goes to private school, so Nate has to deal with that. Perhaps in showing his brother how to handle the teasers, Nate comes to realize how he should handle his own accusers.

Or dealing with a complication may increase the reader's tension because it distracts the character from paying attention to solving the main problem, which the reader can see is getting worse. Suppose Nate also has a job delivering newspapers, and he needs the money to pay for things that the scholarship doesn't cover, like his uniform and school supplies. But someone's stealing his papers, and he has to check his route when he should be trying to identify his accusers. The culprit has nothing to do with the kid who's making trouble for Nate at school, but the reader knows that Nate is spending precious time trying to keep his job, preventing him from taking the time he needs to prove his innocence. This heightens the tension.

The problem and Nate's reaction to it will also influence the other people involved in the plot development. Perhaps his friends turn against him, or one of his parents actually believes he's guilty. Because a novel covers a broader slice of life, look at your character in a larger context, particularly in terms of the relationships he has with other characters.

Read the Pros

1. Read *Warrior Scarlet* by Rosemary Sutcliff. Drem wants to earn the warrior scarlet
   that is his people's badge of manhood, but because of his withered arm he

TRY IT YOURSELF: WHAT'S AT STAKE?

1. Select a character from your character journal whose problem you've identified. Decide how you could intensify the problem to book proportions, and plan a new plot that incorporates this depth.

2. Look at that book plot and think of other problems that your character could face in addition to the main problem. Use these to flesh out your novel.

3. Select one character from your character journal, and make a list of other characters in her life: parents, siblings, neighbors, friends, enemies, teacher, minister, librarian, traffic crossing guard or whoever might interact with that main character. Next to each secondary character, write down how he or she will react to your protagonist's problem.

---

cannot kill his wolf, the physical test that means graduation from the boys' house, despite his attempts to train for the fight. Exiled as a shepherd, Drem learns the true responsibilities of manhood, and when he ultimately kills the same wolf he failed to kill earlier, his accomplishment is not passing a mere test, but a true acknowledgment of his responsibility as one of his people.

2. Read *So You Want to Be a Wizard* by Diane Duane. See how Nita's problem starts out with her simply wanting to cope with classmate bullies. She becomes a wizard to find out how to do this—and in the process she discovers she must take on the responsibility of coping with the worst bully of all: the Lone One, who seeks to destroy balance in the universe.

3. Read . . . *And Now Miguel* by Joseph Krumgold. In the beginning Miguel wants simply to take the sheep up the mountain to prove himself a man. See how he tries to achieve his goal by doing good deeds and finally making wishes to San Ysidro. Miguel's prayer has unexpected consequences, however, and he and his brother grow in understanding the true nature of adulthood by coming to terms with the way the saint answers their prayers.

Variations on a theme

In a short story you only need hint at characters and circumstances beyond the main story situation. If it's a school problem, the reader assumes that the main character has parents (your character may even allude to them by saying something like, "My mom's going to ground me"), but the family probably won't appear in the story. And if it's a church problem, the reader assumes that the kid has a teacher and schoolmate friends that she sees on weekdays, even if they're not part of the action. But a book covers a longer period of time and reflects a larger world. The reader may see the character at school (at least if the story takes place during the school year), at home (unless it's a summer camp story or the kid goes to boarding school), with friends, with family, alone—the whole gamut of life as it develops in the novel. In planning a book, create a believable world for your character in terms of surroundings and people. Most of these secondary characters will be involved in the story action, working to help your character deal with his problem or to hinder him.

These other characters will also have their own problems. Often these will be variations on the book's theme. The theme of *The Proving Ground*, for example, is the importance, and the dangers, of standing up for what you believe. Kevin, the main character, is accustomed to not making waves and keeping a low profile. He must discover how to know when it's the right time to stand up for something and how to judge the consequences—because standing up for what you believe is always done at a cost. In trying to decide when and how to stand up for what he believes, Kevin has to deal with other characters who face the same problem and deal with it in their own way.

★ The antagonist, Duane, has strong beliefs, though they are wrong. His belief is predicated on a misunderstanding based on false knowledge. Duane wants to stand up for what he believes, but he does it in sly, underhanded ways, until the book's climax. At that point, egged on by another character, he takes violent action wildly.

★ As the plot unfolds, Kevin greatly admires Charley, a girl who stands up for what she believes, also. But Duane is her cousin and, like him, she is also standing up for something false. When she learns the truth, however, she stands up with Kevin, against Duane.

★ Kevin's father also stands up for what he believes. He weighs the risks, accepts the consequences and then takes action openly. At the same time, however, he warns Kevin not to take such risks. He wants to keep his son safe—in effect, he wants to keep his son a child. He must accept that Kevin can take his own risks in standing up for his beliefs.

In the course of the book, these other characters grow and change in their understanding of what they believe and how they will act on it, though none as profoundly as Kevin. The reader uses all these variations to bring the theme clearly into focus. In a short story, perhaps there is room for one additional character who reflects the theme as the main character plays it out. The cast of a novel is much richer and, while these additional characters cannot be developed as completely as your viewpoint character, you will need to know them well enough to see how their problems and changes clarify your theme for the reader. You'll discover ways to do this in chapter 11.

Read the Pros

1. Read *Holes* by Louis Sachar. See how every character has holes in his knowledge and understanding. How do the different characters try to fill in those holes? How do they grow and change as a result?
2. Read *The Great Gilly Hopkins* by Katherine Paterson. All the characters want a home and a family, and find (or fail to find) them along the way. Note how Gilly appears to get her wish, but discovers that reality is completely different from what she expected.
3. Read *Wizard's Hall* by Jane Yolen. See how all of the characters try to defeat the sorcerer and his terrifying beast, but Henry tries hardest because he despairs most of having any ability. His trying enables others to succeed.

TRY IT YOURSELF: STORY PROBLEMS

1. Look at the list you made for the previous section of secondary characters and their reactions to the main character's problem. Organize their reactions by: (1) those that reflect positive growth similar to the way the main character will change, (2) those reactions that do not reflect any growth, and (3) those reactions that contrast with the theme that the main character's growth reflects. Select three or four characters who could be significant in a novel based on this character's problem, helping or hindering the character.
2. Select one story problem you've come up with for a character in your character journal. Identify how the character changes and grows in dealing with the problem. Brainstorm a list of ways to deal with such a problem, and decide how you could develop a cast of secondary characters who would encompass those variations.

Unpredictable characters

A novel represents a longer journey of self-discovery for a character. Instead of a single instant of resolution at a story's climax, a book character grows and changes in small ways as the plot develops. This builds to a profound sense of transformation that makes the time the reader invests in the book worthwhile. That transformation will impact the other characters as well. It may also impact the writer.

While you know where you want your plot to go and how you want your character to change and grow, sometimes that character will surprise you along the way. This can happen when a strong idea for a story grabs you and you brainstorm enough information about your character to get you writing, but you don't know everything. Or you think you know your character well, but your plot takes a sudden twist and your character reacts in an unexpected way. The character's reaction makes perfect sense, but it's not what you thought that character would do. It may not even be what you wanted him to do but, if you like this new direction, it will require you to make changes in the rest of your plot from there on.

In *Simon Says*, my main character, Charles, was a painting student at a fine-arts school. He'd gotten impatient with painting dull bowls of fruit for his still life teacher. In a scene that I'd intended to be transitional, I had him finishing a boring still life early so he could spend the rest of his class time on sketches that would be important to the plot later on. I'd already established his frustration with this teacher, however, and Charles surprised me by deciding he was ready to act on it. As I was writing the scene, he wanted to check his painting again. It was drab and lifeless, with the muted colors of the fruit as dull as he remembered them. But instead of turning to those important sketches, Charles didn't want to leave his painting like that. Without completely knowing what he was doing (I certainly didn't know what he was up to), he squeezed some paint onto his palette and began painting something in the front corner of his canvas, on the edge of the table holding the fruit bowl. I let him get on with it, intrigued, and he painted a vivid lemon that shimmered in front of the drab fruit background. With that action, he invested his disgust at the class assignment with a passion expressed in artistic terms that rang true for him, and transformed a place-holding scene into a scene that deepened his character and showed how he was changing and growing.

You can force your character to do what you want, but if you do you'll end up like a puppeteer who's pulling the strings of an inanimate marionette. If you want your characters to live on the page for the reader, let them surprise you and become independent. This may happen because your subconscious has continued to think about the character. You actually know things beyond your character biography that you don't realize you knew. Or this can happen because the character has come to life for you. Follow your character's lead, and let him take charge. This will breathe new life into your story, and energize you as you explore your character in new directions. Readers know that real people are unpredictable, and they will believe your book all the more if the character is human and surprises them as well as surprising you.

 Read the Pros

1. Read *Winter of Magic's Return* by Pamela F. Service. See how the three main characters, Heather, Welly and Merlin, grow and change as they work together to return King Arthur to power in a future ravaged by nuclear war. Service's editor wouldn't accept an early version of this novel, saying that it needed more character depth as the three were influenced by what happened to them in their quest. As she revised the novel, Service was surprised at the depth of Heather's longing to be needed, by how little self-confidence Welly had and by how hard on himself Merlin was. See how these character qualities enhance the novel's impact.

2. Read *Maggie's Wish* by Marilyn Anderson. Bored with the story of a girl and her horse, Anderson found herself writing about a duck one day. She found out that the duck's name was Gracie and that she was a Muscovy—a large, ugly duck with a red ring around her eye. See how Gracie takes over the book. Anderson let her do whatever she wanted, including dive-bombing the neighbors in their swimming pool.

TRY IT YOURSELF: UNPREDICTABLE CHARACTERS

1. Let your character surprise you. When he does, interview him. Ask him why he did what he did, and how this is going to change him. Free-write a monologue in which he answers these questions and talks about his goals. Don't think critically as you write. Set a time limit and write for ten or fifteen minutes without stopping until the limit is up. This will allow the ideas in your subconscious to spill out on paper freely, and you will learn valuable things about your character.

2. Sometimes your character surprises you by not knowing what he wants to do, but making it clear that he doesn't want to behave the way you want him to. Take some time away from your writing, and let your mind wander. Do something physical, like washing dishes, jogging, working out or weeding the garden. While your body is occupied your mind can wander, and your character might tell you what he's thinking. Keep a pad of paper nearby so you can freewrite his thoughts as they come.

3. Sometimes one of your characters just isn't working. Ask yourself some questions to loosen up your thinking about this character:

   ★ How does the character change from the beginning to the end? Is the change believable? If not, what qualities could you give the character to set up this change more effectively?

   ★ If there's no change, why is the story problem imperative to this particular character? If you don't know, why might such a problem matter to a kid? Use the answer to help you establish a motivation for your character.

   ★ Is your character monodimensional? Does he or she have a life outside the story problem? What aspects of that life could relate to the struggle to resolve the problem and develop your character more fully?

   ★ Does your character want to do something different? Perhaps the character seems flat because you're trying to force him or her to do something that doesn't feel right.

   ★ Write a scene where the character talks to someone outside of the main story action. See if your character surprises you in the conversation.

PART III
A Story in Search of a Cast

EXCEPTIONAL CHARACTERS
Heroes and Villains

Kids invest a lot of emotional energy in their reading. They want to love the hero, hate the villain and picture themselves in the hero's role. To make your story live up to their expectations, you need to create exceptional protagonists and exceptional antagonists—but that's not a simple matter of making your protagonist exceptionally perfect and your antagonist exceptionally evil. Both the problem-solver and problem-causer need to be exceptionally well rounded and exceptionally believable for the story to ring true for your reader.

Human heroes

Few readers can identify with Peerless Percival, the perfect hero who is brave, wise, understanding and insightful; who looks attractive and dresses well; who always does the right thing and knows just what to say in any situation. For a start, real kids know they aren't anything like Percival, and never will be, so they have trouble becoming fully involved in his story. And if your hero is truly peerless and able to cope with anything, you'll end up with a very short story, because Percival would know exactly how to solve the story problem in the first scene. Make the situation more challenging for your story hero, and leave him some room to grow and change, by creating a character who is more human and less perfect. What makes a hero heroic is his willingness to face a problem he didn't seek and deal with it—just the way a reader hopes he could actually rise to the occasion in real life. Start with an ordinary kid who finds himself in an extraordinary situation, and give him the willingness to face it.

While you want your hero to be human, you don't want him to be so ordinary that your reader would overlook him in a crowd. To capture your reader's interest, you should make your hero exceptionally engaging: he should engage the reader's curiosity and empathy. You achieve this by using all the building blocks of character craft you've seen in Parts I and II of this book to create a complex character the reader will be drawn to immediately.

Most importantly, your hero shouldn't be too casual about the story problem. He must be exceptionally motivated to face it and deal with it. This is important because the reader will find himself involved in the book in direct proportion to how deeply the hero is driven to handle his situation. Secondary characters may be drawn into the story problem by the main character or by circumstances. They may not really care how it works out as long as they get out of it and get back to their own lives in the end, but your hero needs a greater commitment. He must *need* to resolve the problem and worry that he won't be able to as things get worse. Peerless Percival is unconvincing as a story hero because he strolls through life's tribulations without fear or concern, clothes tidy, hair in place, deftly dispatching antagonists and navigating obstacles as if they were trivial. A ridiculous character like that might make your readers laugh, but he wouldn't hold their interest for long unless you're writing parody or superhero comic strips. A character might start out appearing to be perfect, but something would have to shatter his absolute confidence pretty quickly if you want to make an apparently Peerless Percival convincing as your hero.

The key to creating believable heroes lies in giving them a mixture of strengths and flaws. Like the reader, your hero should have minor problems, such as difficult teachers, pesky siblings and neighbors, secret fears, troubling memories, a yearning for something like the attention of the boy or girl next door—all as part of this character's life before the story problem rears its ugly head and the plot takes off. In other words, your hero must be a quirky, complex character with a past and a hoped-for future that may change with the appearance of the problem.

As you develop your plot, try to stay away from always using the hero's positive qualities to help him solve his story problems and allowing his flaws to hinder him. Real life isn't so neat and tidy. Sometimes good qualities get in the way, while weaknesses prove surprisingly helpful. Perhaps Eva is exceptionally honest—a good quality. But honesty works against her when she's supposed to make up a story to tell her mother so she can sneak out of the house one evening with her best friend. And she's afraid of the dark, a weakness that the other kids make fun of. But when she and her friend decide to explore a dark cave, Eva hangs back, so she's safe when her friend falls into a pit. Now Eva can find a way to rescue her. Let your hero's qualities help or detract in unexpected ways, and you'll create unconventional characters who will appeal to your readers.

Probably the contemporary hero in the most classic mode is Harry Potter of the J.K. Rowling books. When *Harry Potter and the Sorcerer's Stone* begins, Harry has lost his parents, has been mistreated by his aunt and uncle and is clueless about his wizard's heritage. As the first book in the series gets underway he finds himself confused by Hogwarts School of Witchcraft and Wizardry, bullied by Malloy and Snipes, and amazed and delighted by his unexpected skills at the game of Quidditch (rather than conceited, the way Peerless Percival would be). He's uncertain how to find the sorcerer's stone but determined to prevent the dangerous Voldemort from finding it first. Despite his wizard ancestry, Harry is basically an ordinary kid who finds himself in an extraordinary situation and rises to the occasion.

Your hero must prove himself exceptionally willing to follow through on what he starts, using his imagination, his inner strengths (which may surprise him), his quirky individuality and even his flaws to come to terms with the story situation and resolve the problem that faces him. In the end of your story, your hero must be exceptional in one other way—he must be exceptionally open to growth and change. Remember that your main character should change and grow as a result of dealing with the story problem. Peerless Percival is too smug to change—why should he? He's perfect. Your character must accept that he's not perfect and be open to changes in his life, just like the readers who identify with him.

Flawed heroes

Young readers like to read about sympathetic characters who do the right thing under difficult circumstances. Older readers—middle graders and adolescents—may be drawn to less admirable main characters. These readers have their own darker sides, and find it easier to identify with heroes that reflect that. On the surface, it seems as if some heroes shouldn't even be heroes at all.

As I was writing *Counterfeit Son*, Cameron seemed an unusual hero.

The son of a serial killer, abused by his father, Cameron is left alone after his father is killed when police try to arrest him. He decides to pass himself off as one of his father's victims, claiming that he was kept alive all these years. Cameron knew that his father tortured and murdered over twenty boys, yet he never told anyone or helped any of the boys escape. Now he is taking advantage of a new family's longing to have their son back by pretending to be that boy. He's lying to the people who take him into their home and give him their love. This impostor certainly doesn't sound like hero material!

But Cameron's readers know that they lie to people they love, and they feel guilty over things they have let pass or left undone. They identify with Cameron, and empathize with him as he tries to fit into a real family at last. And they accept the lies he tells to the police and to the family. They even accept his stealing from the family in a desperate attempt to pay off an old accomplice of his father's who shows up to blackmail him.

However, if the book ended with Cameron continuing to lie and take deliberate advantage of the family who took him in, the reader would be left unsatisfied. If a hero is deeply flawed, he must find a way to overcome or transcend those flaws at the climax of the story. Cameron ends up risking everything to try to save a new boy from the accomplice, even to the point of admitting that he's an impostor. In doing so he accepts and overcomes his guilt at doing nothing to help the other boys, and earns an honest chance at a new life.

Developing exceptional heroes with profound flaws will engage your readers' concern and sympathy on a deeper level. You can do this to enrich a novel for older readers by creating a complex main character with a dark side that threatens to overwhelm him, then pushing him to the point where he must choose whether or not to give in to it.

 Read the Pros

1. Read *The Maze* by Will Hobbs. See how the death of Rick's grandmother leaves him angry and feeling cut off from society. In his attempt to run away, he instead runs into the isolated camp of a bird biologist in the middle of a maze of canyons, and into an opportunity to make a new start for himself.

2. Read *A Wrinkle in Time* by Madeleine L'Engle. Meg, the main character, seems to have more character faults than admirable qualities in the beginning. Yet by the end of the book, some of those faults enable her to save her father and brother.

TRY IT YOURSELF: HEROES

1. Brainstorm a list of possible strengths your main character might possess. Now brainstorm a list of weaknesses the same character might have. Plan out ways that the strengths could make things difficult for your character and ways the weaknesses could work to the character's advantage.

2. Brainstorm a list of serious character flaws. Choose one or any combination of them, and develop a character who possesses them. Now brainstorm some sympathetic qualities that could make this character an unexpected hero.

3. Brainstorm a list of story problems, and select several that appeal to you as potential story starters. Plan out reasons that a character might be driven to solve that problem. Now give your character a mixture of strengths and weaknesses that will both make the problem tougher for him to solve, and also offer him potential solutions to the problem.

---

3. Read *How the Grinch Stole Christmas* by Dr. Seuss. The Grinch is certainly a hero who looks like a villain in the beginning. But kids can relate to someone who resents other people making noise and bothering him, and makes up his mind to do something about it. See how none of the warmhearted Whos, who already know the true meaning of Christmas, have room for character growth, while the Grinch has plenty of room to grow and change as he discovers what Christmas is all about and then has to save the Whos' Christmas from the results of his own scheming.

What your hero is up against

Your exceptional hero needs an exceptional antagonist to oppose him and generate the story problem or complicate it for him. This antagonist may be another character, but not always. In some stories, circumstances provide the story problem—Ali is searching for hidden treasure, for example. No one stands in her way, but no one knows where it's hidden. Ali needs to find it to help her family, perhaps, or a friend. She is presented with a critical situation and must overcome obstacles to find a solution, but she's not actually up against a villain. In this sort of story you have a protagonist, but no human antagonist for your hero to face. Consequently, all the reader's attention will be focused on the protagonist's quest, and you won't need to create an equally exceptional antagonist to balance your exceptional hero.

In other stories, the antagonist is a force rather than a person. The enemy could be a storm, a flood or the end of the world. If Nature is the enemy, that doesn't always have to imply a disaster story, however. Matthew could struggle to keep the family farm going in spite of a bad drought after his father has been seriously injured. The hot, dry weather is the enemy, and you will have to show it vividly through Matthew's eyes, bringing it to life the way you'd show a human enemy. Let the reader see the high, dry clouds and feel the hot wind. Show Matthew's sickened shock when the well runs dry, and his triumph when the rain finally starts and he knows he can salvage at least some of their crops. You'll have to research natural phenomena to show this sort of antagonist clearly, since you may not know the qualities of Nature as well as you know the qualities a person could possess to make him act a certain way. Or you may be able to use a natural phenomenon you're familiar with. If you live in a place frequented by tornadoes or earthquakes or heavy, flooding rains, for example, you may already know enough to write believably about these natural enemies.

And finally, your hero may discover that what he's up against is actually himself. To resolve his problem, he must face and overcome an inner flaw. This goes beyond the inherent weaknesses that make your characters human. Being cranky is a character weakness, but having a nasty temper that can turn violent could be the story problem that your hero has to face. Suppose Eric has moved to a new town and is worried about starting school in the middle of the year and making new friends. You don't have to introduce a bully who makes Eric's life miserable or even have other kids dislike him—Eric can create the problem himself by letting his temper get the best of him. He might be so worried about the volcano he's building for his science project that he gets mad working on it the night before it's due and smashes it. He might kick the neighbor's dog because it pesters him. Eric could lose his temper so often that even the kids who tried to be friendly in the beginning turn against him. To fit in, Eric has to learn how to handle that temper.

The enemy can also turn out to be a handicap or illness—the heroine must accept that her body has betrayed her. Coping with sudden blindness or deafness, with an illness such as cancer or AIDS, or with a birth condition such as cerebral palsy or ADD, forces the main character to reassess the goals and dreams that most kids take for granted. As with

Nature, you'll have to do some serious research to write about this sort of antagonist. Your description of symptoms, treatment and coping mechanisms must be accurate. At the climax of the story, your heroine should find a way to accept her limitations and transcend them in order to come to terms with herself and move forward with her life.

Whether you give your hero a human or a nonhuman antagonist, always be aware that the enemy in the story must take on a life of its own and be well developed to stand believably against your exceptional hero.

Read the Pros

1. Read *Magic Elizabeth* by Norma Kassirer. Sally has no real villain to face in this mystery. Instead, she has to come to terms with staying with an elderly, distant aunt. She does so by passing through a magic mirror to another time in search of a long-lost doll, and by trying to help a mysterious girl who appears and needs a friend.
2. Read *Hatchet* by Gary Paulsen. See how Nature becomes the antagonist as Brian struggles to survive alone in the Canadian wilderness after the plane taking him to visit his father crashes.
3. Read *From Anna* by Jean Little. See how Anna struggles to adapt to her eye problems as she tries to settle into her new home after her family emigrates to Canada from Europe.

TRY IT YOURSELF: VILLAINS

1. Think of a an aspect of Nature that you're familiar with and that you find threatening, such as thunderstorms or a deserted stretch of cliffs overlooking the ocean. Plan out how you might put a character in conflict with this. Decide what combination of strengths and weaknesses your character will bring to the situation.
2. Choose an illness or physical disability, and create a character who must deal with the condition. Decide whether your character tries to deny it, uses it as an excuse to avoid doing certain things, reacts with anger or with tears, or does something else entirely. Write a scene in which your character finally confronts the truth and finds a way to come to terms with it.

Sympathetic villains

In most stories your hero will face an enemy who creates the story problem or complicates the issue for the antagonist. Although you will show this enemy through the main character's perspective, you need to develop your antagonist in as much detail as you develop your hero. For a start, give your villain some redeeming characteristics. Perhaps Evil Evelyn steals candy from children on Halloween and kicks their kittens the rest of the year. But she volunteers to help the new kid in class with math homework, and she always stops and says hello to the elderly man who runs the corner newsstand, brightening his day. Instead of flat out disliking her, both the reader and the protagonist will now feel off-balance about Evelyn, uncertain as to what sort of person she really is.

Your villain must also have motivation and be able to engage the reader's sympathy for his actions in at least some small way. For example, my antagonist in *The Proving Ground* is a vicious, violent kid. Duane gouges the paint jobs on cars that have a parking sticker from the local military base, and he threatens the hero, Kevin, with a switchblade the first time they meet. Duane's hatred of the military escalates to the point where he plans to blow up the deserted military base—and Kevin along with it. It might seem difficult to give him any redeeming characteristics. But I asked myself why a kid might want to do that. I used a combination of Duane's fear of never amounting to anything and the effect of peer pressure on him to create a believable antagonist.

Duane has bragged so long that he would get even with the military for stealing his family farm that he's afraid he'll end up a laughing stock unless he makes good on his threat. And a "friend" at school feeds that insecurity, ragging on Duane until he believes the only thing he can do is take decisive action. When Kevin discovers his plan, Duane feels he has no choice but to force Kevin to participate or to kill him if he refuses, something that never crossed his mind before his attack on the base. In this case, Duane's weakness helped build character sympathy for him—readers could imagine being goaded into doing something they didn't really want to do, and then losing themselves in it as things get out of control.

As with your hero, make your antagonist exceptionally believable. Evil Evelyn, with her candy stealing and kitten kicking, will certainly be easy for your reader and your protagonist to hate if she acts out of pure meanness—but older readers, at least, know that kids usually have some reason for acting bad. They expect to see that same sort of reason in the stories and books they read. As you develop your villains, give them a reason in their own mind that justifies their actions. If Evil Evelyn kicks other kids' kittens, ask yourself why. Maybe her parents drowned the stray kitten she brought home, saying that kittens were dirty and carried disease and she should know better. Evelyn felt she couldn't hate her parents for being so cruel to her and to the kitten, so she turned her hatred on other kittens belonging to other children.

Your protagonist still has to deal with Evelyn in order to keep her own kitten safe, but Evelyn has become more believable—and perhaps more dangerous. A two-dimensional antagonist who has meanness without motive is a cardboard villain the hero should be able to knock down with a flick of the hand. A complex antagonist who acts out of desperation and pain will be harder to handle and more satisfying to overcome—or perhaps even redeem—in the end. If you create compelling heroes and villains in your fiction, you'll sweep readers into the tension of your story problem, and carry them through your plot to its resolution.

As a result of that resolution, your antagonist may change, just as your protagonist changes—for the better, or even for the worst. Perhaps your protagonist's attitude toward the antagonist changes, and the resolution comes about because the protagonist no longer feels the antagonist is his enemy. The reader's attitude toward the antagonist may change as well. By making these two pivotal characters more complex, you will deepen your plot, and deepen your readers' experiences as they share these characters' lives. But the hero and the antagonist are only part of your cast. You will see how to develop them further through their relationships with secondary characters in the next chapter.

 Read the Pros

1. Read *Bat 6* by Virginia Euwer Wolff. See how Shazam unforgivably attacks Aki, a ball player of Japanese heritage on the opposing team, during a community softball game in 1949. Despite the viciousness of her attack, readers can sympathize with Shazam because she has been traumatized after her father was killed in the Japanese bombing of Pearl Harbor.

2. Read *Never Trust a Dead Man* by Vivian Vande Velde. After Selwyn's enemy, Farold, gets murdered, Selwyn is accused of the murder and walled up alive with the corpse. When a quirky witch resurrects Farold, the two old enemies

TRY IT YOURSELF: SYMPATHETIC VILLAINS

1. Brainstorm a list of villainous actions a kid might take. Beside each one, write a motivation that would explain that action. Choose one combination that appeals most to you, and plan how you might use it to portray an antagonist in a story.

2. Look back at the plot scenarios you developed in Part II, and choose one that has a strong antagonist. Strengthen that antagonist's motivation, and give him some redeeming characteristics. See how this enhances your story as your antagonist begins to balance the believability of your protagonist.

3. Look over the resolution scenes in your story plots. Select one in which the antagonist remains the same at the end as she was at the beginning. Decide how the antagonist might change for the better because of the protagonist's actions—and how she might change for the worse. Try writing both new endings, and see which one strengthens your story more.

---

must work together to find the real murderer—who turns out to be something of a surprising villain as well.

3. Read *Follow My Leader* by James B. Garfield. When Jimmy is blinded by a firecracker, he must deal with Mike, the boy who threw it and who taunts Jimmy's Seeing Eye dog. But see how the author sets up Mike as a sympathetic villain who threw the firecracker out of fear. Later, Mike tried to make friends with Jimmy's dog only to be rebuffed, so he turns to taunting out of guilt and embarrassment. In the end, the real enemy turns out to be Jimmy's blindness and his resentment of it, and his resolution is more coming to terms with his blindness than coming to terms with Mike.

CHAPTER 11

THE REST OF THE GANG

Secondary Characters

Your hero and villain are surrounded by a host of secondary characters who are also involved in the story problem. Some of these kids will be friends of the villain and will work against the main character, making it harder for him to solve the problem. Others will be friends of the protagonist and may be able to help him deal with the situation. And some kids won't care one way or the other in the beginning of the story, but will be drawn into the problem as the plot develops, and may end up choosing sides.

These secondary characters are your protagonist's and antagonist's schoolmates, neighbors, teammates, siblings and playmates. Some of them are merely placeholders—characters you need to move your plot along, but who don't really figure in your story and should simply appear when needed and then disappear, such as a bus driver or a crossing guard. You can give them defining characteristics (the driver wears a thick hand-knitted scarf wrapped several times around her neck and calls out the stops in a hoarse croak because she caught a cold, or the crossing guard marches out to halt traffic as if he were a soldier on parade), but they don't have to be fully developed characters because the reader will see them once and then move on.

You must keep your cast tight in a short story. You might not waste space describing the driver or the crossing guard at all, and use only a few characteristics to show even the other secondary characters. In a novel, however, you have the space to reflect your main character's world more completely, so develop these secondary characters in depth.

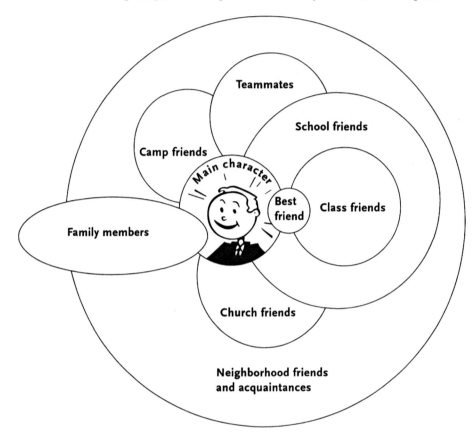

The hero's right hand

In most books and stories, you'll want to give your hero a best friend or a character who is deeply involved in the situation along with the hero, someone who may grow into a best friend before the story is over. This character is important, because it gives the protagonist someone to talk to (allowing you to show some of the story through dialogue, which readers love). This friend also supplies someone who will offer the protagonist a sympathetic ear and practical assistance once things start going wrong. The best friend is loyal and true, and cares about resolving the story problem nearly as much as the hero does. This character is also in a position to challenge the hero and to criticize him more freely than other characters can. Since the hero will listen to his best friend, this character can make the protagonist face unwelcome truths. Because your reader will see a great deal of this friend, develop him or her almost as fully as you develop the main character.

As with your own relationships, the two characters should have something in common to generate their friendship, but may have quite a few differences that complicate it. If Briana's best friend is Shannon because they live next door to each other, decide what things they do together—and what they don't. Maybe they play board games but the only outdoor games they both like are swimming and playing on the swings. When kids choose sides for kickball at recess, Briana is eager to play but Shannon isn't, so Shannon is left alone while her best friend has a great time with the other kids.

If Briana's story problem looms during the kickball game, Shannon may not even find out about it until later, and her reaction may be colored by the fact that she isn't part of the game and doesn't plan to ever become part of it. In fact, Shannon may fear that she'll lose her position as Briana's best friend because Briana's so involved in what's happening during recess kickball games.

A best friend can also betray the hero. When Briana and Shannon quarrel, perhaps Shannon defects to the enemy's side, sharing secrets that Briana would rather not have revealed. Or perhaps Shannon is hurt, but not mad enough to rat on Briana. Instead, she fails to show up at a crucial moment, leaving Briana to face imminent disaster on her own. To solve her story problem, Briana must also patch up her friendship.

Sometimes that isn't possible. Sometimes the hero and her best friend are so far apart that they can't stay friends after the story's resolution. Suppose the problem is that Briana wants to join the school soccer team—kickball is only for recess fun. The school board insists it's a boys-only team, but Briana's parents encourage her and say that unless the school starts a girls-only team, they have to let Briana play on the school team. Briana is determined to play, and she expects her best friend to support her.

But why isn't Shannon playing kickball in the first place? Perhaps her parents disapprove of girls playing sports, especially with boys. As Briana's situation escalates, Shannon's parents go to the school board meeting to insist that girls like Briana not be allowed on the school team. They forbid Shannon to play with Briana anymore. Does Shannon think her parents are right? Will she obey them? Does she long to play soccer herself, or does she wish Briana wouldn't play rough sports with boys? Perhaps Briana's determination to get on the team brought the differences between them to a head, and Shannon decides that *she* doesn't want to be friends with Briana any longer, regardless of what her parents think.

It can also be revealing if your hero doesn't have a best friend. An isolated main character will be more vulnerable. If Briana's a loner who makes a stink about joining the boys-only soccer team, the other kids on the team and the members of the school board might think there's something wrong with her because she doesn't fit in anywhere. Without a friend to trust, Briana might even question herself and wonder if this is what she really wants.

In stories for middle graders or adolescents, the best friend may be a girlfriend or boyfriend. That makes the tensions between the two of them potentially even more volatile. Briana wants to play on the middle-school soccer team. Her boyfriend has always liked playing soccer with her and the other neighborhood kids, but he's also on the team and all the other guys are teasing him because it's his girl who's trying to crash their locker room. Briana expects his support, but he may feel pressured in too many directions and won't be able to give it.

Sometimes these two characters don't even start out as friends, but the circumstances of the book bring them together. This can work particularly well if you write your story from two different viewpoints, switching back and forth from one character to another. Perhaps another girl wants to play on the team also, but has never done anything about it. At a critical moment, she chooses to stand with Briana, and the two of them refuse to give up. Or one of the boys on the team might decide that Briana deserves a tryout as much as any other kid and breaks ranks with his teammates to support Briana's demand to join the team.

However this friendship occurs or however it ends, that relationship will be one of the most important in your story, right up with the relationship between the protagonist and antagonist. Develop your hero's best friend with care. He can be a bridge between the reader and your main character as he voices questions, doubts and support that the reader shares.

Read the Pros

1. Read *Amber Brown Is Not a Crayon* by Paula Danziger. Note how Amber and Justin are sometimes worst enemies and sometimes best friends as they try to survive third grade together.

2. Read *A Separate Peace* by John Knowles. See how Gene and Phinny are best friends—who turn out to not know each other at all.

3. Read *The View From Saturday* by E.L. Konigsburg. See how Noah, Nadia, Ethan

TRY IT YOURSELF: FIND A FRIEND

1. Take a character you've developed in your character journal and give him or her a best friend. Decide why they're friends and what they like about each other. Also decide what they'd each like to change about the other. Write a scene in which they argue over something. Are they still friends after the argument is over?

2. Select a story where you've given the main character a strong best friend. Write a scene in which the friend decides to turn against the main character. Does this strengthen your story?

3. Choose a story in which your main character has a best friend who's always supportive. Rewrite the story without the friend. How does this affect the protagonist's growth at the end?

---

and Julian come together to fill the gaps in each other's lives and merge to form not only a winning sixth-grade Academic Bowl team, but also a complex friendship.

4. Read *Armageddon Summer* by Jane Yolen and Bruce Coville. Marina and Jed meet only after their parents take them to a remote mountain retreat where the Believers plan to watch the end of the world from safety. Confused by what's going on at the retreat, Marina and Jed find themselves working together to save the cult's children from its leaders. See how the authors write alternating chapters from the different characters' perspective. It's interesting to note that Yolen did not simply write Marina's chapter while Coville wrote Jed's chapters—the book was a true collaboration.

Hang out with a sidekick

A best friend doesn't always have to be a serious relationship—sometimes that friend can be a sidekick who makes the reader laugh. Or the hero can have both a best friend and a humorous sidekick. Humor can be a wonderful way to draw a reader into a story. When kids laugh, their emotions open up. Shared humor makes the reader bond more tightly with the protagonist than shared suffering. Kids put up defenses against pain and these defenses can distance your readers from the heart of your protagonist's growth and transformation. Kids rarely put up defenses against laughter, however—the more the better. And once readers let their defenses sag by laughing, they're more open to the character's suffering and growth.

TRY IT YOURSELF: CREATE A SIDEKICK

1. Take a serious hero you've written about in your character journal. Create a sidekick friend for him who comments on the action. Give this sidekick a sense of humor. Write a scene in which the hero confronts the antagonist, and use the sidekick to needle the antagonist.
2. Choose a story situation you've planned out that has a dramatic climax. Give your hero a sidekick, and rewrite the climax scene from the sidekick's point of view as he or she participates in it. Use the humor to emphasize the underlying theme of the story.
3. Choose an unconventional sidekick such as a quirky cousin, a pet or an adult. Write a scene showing the relationship between the protagonist and the sidekick using dialogue and action.

Some sidekicks are the actual story narrators. They tell the reader about this great friend of theirs and his escapades, and help the reader see what's actually going on more clearly because of their wry comments or honest bemusement at what that great friend has gotten the two of them into. A sidekick helps the writer find a quirky way of looking at the story action and the characters by standing just outside of them. Kids often feel like outsiders—strangers in a strange land who worry they won't measure up to the kids they admire and fear being classed with the nerds they despise. Readers will have no trouble identifying with a sidekick who's also an outsider, but who has a special perspective on the main character.

You develop your sidekicks much the way you develop the hero's more serious best friend, but with a lighter touch. Whereas Briana needs Shannon's support and would be bereft if it were suddenly withdrawn, her sidekick could be a gum-cracking kid who would never dream of playing soccer herself but thinks it's fine if Briana wants to do it. Maybe the sidekick throws balls out for Briana to practice kicking, but refuses to chase them. If Briana wants this so much, she can run after the balls while the sidekick sits in a lawn chair eating cookies and listening to her radio.

Sometimes sidekicks can take the fall for the main character. Because the team is being so unfriendly, Briana decides to sneak into the locker room and squirt shaving cream into all the boys' lockers—and she gets her sidekick to help her. The sidekick's can of shaving cream jams and she's got to stop to clear the nozzle, so she falls behind and is still spraying when the coach comes in and finds her. Having the sidekick take the rap makes Briana even more determined—both to get on the team and to make people realize that she won't give up. A responsible best friend might not be willing to help Briana with the prank, and she probably wouldn't let herself get caught. But a sidekick can mess up and make the reader laugh while underlining the seriousness of how the situation is escalating.

 Read the Pros

1. Read *Soup 1776* by Robert Newton Peck. See how the narrator, Rob, is Soup's sidekick and often makes the point for the reader in the face of his friend's escapades as the two tackle revisionist history in their Vermont town.
2. Read *Winnie-the-Pooh* by A.A. Milne. See how Piglet serves as Pooh's sidekick. Piglet's perceptions, actions and comments help put Pooh and the situation in the Hundred Acres Wood in perspective for the reader.
3. Read *Bunnicula: A Rabbit-Tale of Mystery* by Deborah Howe and James Howe. Chester is the main character, who suspects that the baby rabbit rescued by their human family is actually a vampire (possibly because of his pointy fangs and his nocturnal habits). See how Harold, the narrator, serves as Chester's scoffing sidekick. Mysteries often feature sidekicks: In the Encyclopedia Brown series by Donald J. Sobol, partner Sally Kimball serves as the young detective's sidekick.
4. Read *A Taste of Daylight* by Crystal Thrasher. See how sidekicks can be siblings as well as friends.

Family position

Beyond a best friend or sidekick and the antagonist, your hero is part of a variety of groups. First, he's a member of his family, which may be a large group if he has siblings, aunts, uncles, cousins and grandparents. Take birth order into account when exploring your character's family—is the hero an only child, the first born, the baby of the family or somewhere in the middle? Sociologists have linked certain behavior patterns with a child's birth order. Only children are often logical, self-centered, critical perfectionists who act like small adults. First-born children sometimes exhibit the same behavior as only children, being hard-driven, assertive high achievers. Some first-born kids, however, are compliant students and nurturing caregivers. They're so eager to please others that they can be taken advantage of. These kids may nurse their resentments quietly and then explode.

Last-born children are often clowns who entertain everyone, partly

TRY IT YOURSELF: FAMILY AND NEIGHBORS

1. Choose one main character from your character journal and develop his or her family. Decide on their ages and their attitudes toward the protagonist and the story problem. How does adding them in or taking them out affect your story?
2. Create a set of classmates surrounding your main character in a school story. Write a one-paragraph sketch of each one, showing how he or she feels about the character and the story problem.
3. Give your protagonist a group of cabin mates in a camp story. Pick several campers who reflect different attitudes toward the main character's situation. Write a confrontation between your protagonist and one camper who dislikes this hero. Will the hostile camper change his or her mind?
4. Go beyond your character's main circle of friends to look at a larger circle of neighbors or acquaintances. Write a scene in which one of these characters surprises your protagonist by unexpectedly supporting him or her. Let the motivation for this support become clear through the dialogue.

---

because they live in the shadow of their older brothers and sisters and aren't taken seriously. These kids can be impetuous because they're determined to make their mark somehow. Children born in the middle are something of a paradox—they may compete with their older brothers and sisters, or they may grow in entirely different directions so as to avoid competition. These kids tend to hang out with friends more than with their family. When you give your hero brothers and sisters, pay attention to the implications of each one's birth order position.

In and out of class

Your hero is also a member of his neighborhood, including both the kids and the adults he sees regularly. He's a member of his class at school. He may be a member of a youth group at church or temple. He may be a member of a sports team, club or even a gang. The other members of these groups will figure into the action. Even in a novel, you can't develop every one of these kids fully, however, or you'd have no room for plot or description. So you have to zero in on one significant facet of each character: how that character relates to your hero and his problem.

To find these groups, start with your protagonist and radiate out. Briana wants to play on the soccer team. Immediately you know that the guys on the team will be involved in her story. Some will think she's crazy, some may be a little scared of her, some may hate her, some may think she's funny, some may secretly (or not so secretly) sympathize. You can't develop every member of the team, but you can zero in on a few who exemplify each attitude. Show how these players act on their reactions, and then give them a couple of other qualities that round them out.

Perhaps the guy who hates Briana for wanting to play on the team has a little sister he baby-sits at night because their mother works on the night shift at the factory. He's a nice guy, even responsible, and kind to his little sister, but he feels threatened by a girl who wants to be his equal. The guy who thinks Briana is funny is just playing soccer for the fun of it himself, and he's not the greatest player so the others laugh at him a lot. He figures she just wants to play for fun, too, and he kind of likes the idea of having somebody else for the rest of the team to laugh at. You don't have to give the reader a lot of background on each of these characters—just enough to make them stand out from the crowd.

In addition to the team, Briana's classmates will be involved because the story takes place at school. Some of them will support her, some will think she's crazy, some will try to stop her and some won't care. Again, choose representative characters and develop them enough so the reader can recognize and believe in them. In addition to showing their views and giving them some motivation for their attitudes, you might give them some sort of tag that helps pin them down for the reader—Phil's always combing his hair, Angie stutters, Carl says "awesome" almost every time he opens his mouth. These groups can overlap as well—Carl may be in Briana's class and also on the soccer team.

Beyond the school world, Briana has parents who support her and neighbors who do and others who don't. She may have friends from camp, where she first learned to play soccer. She has the school board to face down. Perhaps the local newspaper sends a reporter who decides to champion her—or tries to embarrass her. Like the rings that spread out from a pebble in a clear lake, the cast of characters spreads out from your main character. And as the rings grow fainter as they get farther from the pebble, the characters farther away from Briana and her problem are the placeholders that merit only a simple defining characteristic rather than in-depth characterization.

Read the Pros

1. Read *Meet the Austins* by Madeleine L'Engle. See how the author shows the Austin family as an important circle of characters spreading out from Vicky.
2. Read the *Polk Street School* series by Patricia Reilly Giff. See how the author shows the circle of school friends.
3. Read *Slot Machine* by Chris Lynch. See how the author shows the group of boys struggling to find their slots in different sports teams during a difficult summer retreat prior to starting Catholic school.

Group dynamics

Whether the rest of the cast is made up of school friends, teammates or fellow worshipers from church, the group will become a character in its own right. Even though the team is made up of distinct members who may feel differently about Briana individually, the team has its own personality. If they have a winning record, perhaps their personality is confident or even cocky. That attitude will color their reactions toward Briana. If they're at the bottom of the standings, the team personality may be defeatist. They may feel they're such losers, they deserve to be stuck with a problem like Briana. Or they may feel that enough is enough—they're sick of getting dumped on—and freeze her out.

Often the group's personality is determined by a leader—the kid the others all look up to, who may or may not be the team captain. There's also a would-be leader eager to take the other's place in the hierarchy. There are the newbies, who get no respect, and the members who have been there the longest and who have the choice lockers and get first crack at the showers.

Sometimes the hierarchy of friendships isn't based merely on how long kids have been a part of it. A small knot of friends may center around the leader, to the point where others yearn to belong but feel almost like outsiders even though they're members of the group as a whole. In a sports team like the soccer team Briana wants to join, there will also be the heroes who are the best players (even though they may not actually be the leaders) and the goats who try hard but are klutzes on the field.

And when Briana shows up for the first time, the mood of the team could well approach a mob mentality if the natural leader and his circle of friends don't want her there, no matter what the school board says. They could freeze her out, refusing to speak to her or pass her the ball.

TRY IT YOURSELF: GROUP DYNAMICS

1. Take a class group in a school story you've written. Plan how individual members react to the main character's attempts to resolve the story problem. Then write a scene in which they turn against the protagonist as a group.

2. Select a sports team that one of your characters joins. Decide which players like the character, which ones don't and which ones hardly notice him. Write a scene in which the entire team surprises itself by coming together to support him.

3. Develop a group or club in which one of the leaders abuses his authority over the other members. Write a scene in which your main character tries to convince the group to elect a new leader.

They could make her life miserable, pouring water in her locker to soak her books and school clothes. Even the players who didn't really mind if she joined may find themselves going along with the group, rather than standing alone or, worse, standing with Briana and becoming a victim instead of one of the inner circle.

Once you expand your hero's circles of friends, develop each group's personality as well as the personality of individuals in the group. And remember that an antagonist may be part of his or her own group also. Perhaps Briana's real enemy isn't a member of the soccer team, but the daughter of a right-wing school board member. She and her group of friends could criticize Briana and embarrass her, hoping to discourage her. Having the antagonist be a part of a group that doesn't radiate from the hero's group will intensify the problem for the protagonist as she's got to be on the lookout for the whole group, not just her enemy.

Read the Pros

1. Read *The Chocolate War* by Robert Cormier. See how group dynamics operate as Archie Costello's secret society, the Vigils, rules Jerry's Catholic school under the protection and domination of Brother Leon.

2. Read *Sixth Grade Secrets* by Louis Sachar. See how Laura and Gabriel start rival secret clubs because of a misunderstanding. The author's insight into school groups is right on target. Also read Sachar's *The Boy Who Lost His Face* and see how David is so determined to join the popular crowd at school that he

goes along with attacking an elderly woman who apparently puts a curse on him in retaliation.

3. Read *The Trial of Anna Cotman* by Vivien Alcock. Anna is overjoyed to be included in the secret Society of the Masks until a new leader becomes abusive to the younger members of the society. When she stands up for them, the entire group turns against her, and puts Anna on trial.

Who's who? Naming your character

Since you have less room to develop your secondary characters, use every opportunity to jump-start them in your reader's mind. The name you give a character helps your reader get an instant impression of his or her personality. A boy named Arthur will probably make your readers think of a noble leader. Caprice or Arabesque conjure an aura of music, and could be the name of a composer's daughter or the nickname of a girl who longs to be a ballet dancer. A boy who blows up his experiment in chemistry class could earn the nickname of Bunsen from his classmates, and earn a chuckle from your readers.

A strong name also helps the reader think about your character on multiple levels. You could name a clever kid Wiley. But maybe underneath that cleverness, he's sly. If that quality is important to your plot, his name will already have planted that suspicion in the reader's mind. You can also let your theme inspire the names of your characters. If your book is about the disillusionment kids feel with American government, you might name your characters for presidents—Carter, Ford and Lincoln.

Unusual names will also make it easier for a reader to recognize a particular secondary character in your stories. Instead of Billy, Susy, Tom and Jane, try naming your characters Lukas, Moira, Krystal or Cher. Play with conventional spelling to transform conventional names into more interesting names for your characters. Try using Jere for Jerry or Hana instead of Hannah.

And both names count. You might name your class president Victoria. But is she a bossy leader, or is she caring? If her last name is Shepherd, your reader won't be surprised when her politicking takes second place to her concern for her classmates. Your name can also have special meanings for special readers. I knew a lot of kids from military families would read *The Proving Ground*, so I chose Spencer as Kevin's surname, to conjure the idea of the Spencer Repeating Rifle. Since his father was in charge of firearms proof testing at the military base, Lt. Colonel Spencer created the impression of someone who might be an expert in this field.

Names can also change as characters change. In *The Ghost Cadet*, Benjy is trying hard to grow up. His mother and sister call him Benjy,

144

TRY IT YOURSELF: NAME YOUR CHARACTER

1. Compile a list of contemporary names in your character journal. Here are some places to look for them:
   * Check newspapers for published honor rolls, sports teams, choir or band trips.
   * Check birth announcements for baby names.
   * Listen to the names parents call their children (at family restaurants, the park, the library, etc.).
2. Look through your character journal for characters who seem too full of themselves. Think about nicknames you could give to cut them down to size. Make a list of potential nicknames that could embarrass a kid. Then make a list of potential fond nicknames their friends might think of.
3. Make a list of names that have variations, like Michael, Mike and Mikey. Set this list aside to use in future stories where you want to emphasize a character's changing impression of himself or other characters's different impressions of him.
4. Take a character whose name you don't like. Make a list of this character's dominant characteristics. Go through a baby name book, and make a list of names whose meanings reflect those characteristics. See if one of those names sounds right to you.

---

which makes him feel like a little kid. When he meets his grandmother, she calls him Benjamin, which feels hard and stiff to him. When he befriends a ghost, however, the ghost calls him Ben, and after Benjy finally achieves his quest and helps the ghost, he takes Ben as the name he has grown into. Sometimes the character will choose a variation of his or her own name. In *The Proving Ground*, Charlene is not your typical sweet, young girl—she feels passionate about causes and beats up boys she doesn't like. Charlene likes people to call her Charley. When Kevin gets angry at her, he wants to call her Chuck. You can do this with your character by choosing a name that works in several ways. Let the variations reflect how other characters see this character and how he sees himself as his story develops.

If you can't think of a name for your character or if you choose something arbitrary like Bobby or Susy, you probably don't know your character well enough yet. Think about the character traits you want to emphasize, and flip through the pages of a baby name book, paying attention to the meanings behind the names. If Jane is a know-it-all who always expects the worse and seems to be right, change her name to Cassie. Kids who have been reading mythology in school will recognize Cassandra right away, and you may play with the idea of a doomsayer to flesh out her personality. Don't get too clever, though. If you choose a name with a subtle meaning that readers have no way of recognizing, you haven't actually illuminated the character at all.

Finally, be sure that the name works for you, because you'll have to live with it for the life of your writing project. A name for your hero should have a positive connotation for you—perhaps a name you associate with someone you admire or a friend from your past. If you arbitrarily give your main character a name you can't stand, you may have trouble liking your hero as you write your book. Save the names with negative connotations for your antagonists. Just the way a character's name must make a personal connection with your reader, it must also be meaningful to you.

 Read the Pros

1. Look at the interesting names authors give their characters, such as Miracle in *Dancing on the Edge* by Han Nolan, and the thieves, Neezer and Lucky, and their virtual slave boy, Beetle, in *The Twin in the Tavern* by Barbara Brooks Wallace. Think about the instant impressions you get of the characters from these names.

2. See the quirky nicknames authors give their characters, such as Worm in *You Can Call Me Worm* by Dan Haas; Wart as the young King Arthur in *The Sword in the Stone* by T.H. White; and Sport, which both Calvin and Charles Wallace call each other (referring to a biological oddity instead of a sports fan) in *A Wrinkle in Time* by Madeleine L'Engle. See how these nicknames give readers an immediate impression of the character.

3. Read *Winter of Magic's Return* by Pamela F. Service. See how Welly's parents named him Wellington, expecting him to grow up to be a strong general. No one calls him Wellington, however—plump and in need of thick glasses, his name has been reduced to Welly. In England, where the book is set, galoshes are called wellies, and the character's schoolmates have reduced him from a brave commander to a squelchy pair of rain boots.

Kids from other cultures

Not all your fiction characters will live in your neighborhood or come from the same cultural background you do. Many urban schools have a student body made up of diverse cultures, and some kids don't even speak English. You may want to integrate these kids into your stories.

One way to do this is to write from the outside looking in. In other words, start with a main character who comes from your own cultural background, and have him or her meet a youngster from a different culture. As the main character discovers the culture, so will the reader. But you still have to draw those other characters from different cultures believably. It's not enough to name one character Jimmy and one character Juan and expect that to take care of the multicultural aspect of your story. A character's ethnic identity must grow out of the heart of what you're writing. Never rely on cultural stereotypes to develop your characters, or you'll insult your readers with unbelievable characterization.

How do you write about other cultures, then? They may not be as far from your experience as you think. Your parents or grandparents may have come from another country that you have never seen. Nevertheless, their culture belongs to you also—you just have to get to know it. Talk to family members about their "quaint" habits, and draw them out about customs that reflect their culture. Think about what life was like for them and how they felt. Use those experiences and feelings to create a character who reflects that culture.

You can also write about a completely different culture from your own. After all, a male writer can write about a girl character, and a human writer can write about a horse character. A combination of research and intuitive imagination will allow you to put yourself in someone else's shoes. You can't write believably about a Harlem teenager or a Kansas farm girl if you're locked in a suburban Los Angeles mentality—not everyone hangs out at the mall or veges out in front of the television. Let go of your expectations that all families are like yours, and immerse yourself in a different world.

It helps tremendously to have lived in a culture, even if you were an outsider, or to know someone from the culture you're writing about. If you have lived and worked side by side with people of another culture, you've developed insights into the thoughts and feelings that make them unique. This will allow you to create convincing characters. It will also help to ask your friends to read about the character you've developed, if you feel comfortable doing this. Their feedback on how believable the character seems to them may help you correct misunderstandings that could lead to undesirable stereotyping or other insulting characterization. Accuracy is essential. A mistake in ethnic characterization could hurt or anger readers from that culture or reinforce erroneous stereotypes.

Celebrate the uniqueness of each culture you write about, even while you zero in on the universality of the human experience. You'll end up with characters that speak to readers of all cultures.

TRY IT YOURSELF: OTHER CULTURES, OTHER WORLDS

1. Talk to family members or read old family letters or diaries to get some insight into the culture your parents or grandparents grew up in. Make note of special phrases or customs that can help bring that world to life. Imagine these family members as kids.

2. Plan a vacation that takes you into a different world—perhaps you might visit the Amish country or explore an urban barrio. Talk to young people and make notes in your character journal about the similarities and differences you see between them and the kids from your own culture. Observe more than one youngster so you can see differences between them and avoid stereotypes.

3. Find out if your local high school hosts a foreign exchange student. If so, do some advance research about the student's home country and then arrange to meet the student. Talk to him or her about his culture. Go home and write a brief sketch of a fictional character from that country. Ask the student to read it and ask for honest feedback on what you've captured and what you've misunderstood.

Read the Pros

1. Read *Sees Behind Trees* by Michael Dorris. See how the author captures a sixteenth-century Powhatan youth who yearns to prove himself despite his poor eyesight. The youth discovers that the most difficult truths force you to see beyond the surface rather than simply seeing into the distance.

2. Read *Ghost Train* by Paul Yee. Choon-yi's father goes to North America to work on building the railroad and summons his daughter to join him. When Choon-yi arrives, however, she discovers that he has died, and he wants her to find a way to help him return his soul to China. See how the author draws on his own feelings about immigrating from China to North America to write this vivid story.

3. Read *Park's Quest* by Katherine Paterson. Park's father died in Vietnam before his son had a chance to know him. When Park journeys to his grandfather's farm, trying to learn about his father, he discovers instead a Vietnamese family that has come to America. See how he begins to see their culture, and discover his own father as well.

ANIMALS, ALIENS AND SERIES CHARACTERS

Special Characters for
Special Situations

Some characters will play special roles in your writing and might not follow the conventions of character growth through plot resolution. These may be inanimate objects that become characters in your story, or animals, robots or other special types of creatures that figure in different genres. Series characters that appear in book after book will grow and change in different ways because of their return appearances. While you use many of the same techniques to create appealing, interesting and believable characters in these roles, you'll also need to keep some special considerations in mind.

Characters that hang around

Series characters can't reach a profound moment of growth and change at the climax of each book because they're part of a longer ongoing story. You can write several different sorts of series. For example, J.K. Rowling's Harry Potter books are a series of seven books that were conceived as a single story broken down into seven parts, one for each year Harry spends at Hogwarts, the wizard boarding school. Some series are bound together by theme and place, such as C.S. Lewis's Chronicles of Narnia series. These books feature different human characters who are drawn into the realm of Narnia to help Aslan achieve victory. Other series, such as

Animorphs, Nancy Drew and The Baby-Sitters Club, are never-ending series of books written by different authors under the name of the original author. Each book is a new adventure featuring familiar characters, and the series could end at any time or, in the case of a series like Nancy Drew, could apparently go on endlessly. It's not possible to have the main character go through a major life change at the climax of each book. But some of the aspects of character development remain the same.

You still need to create well-rounded characters for the group of continuing kids that appear in every book. Kids love series books because they feel the characters in them are like friends, and they can't wait to see what their friends are up to next. For these characters to become much-loved friends, they must be fully developed and diverse. While a single novel will have one main character, a series is usually about a group of characters united by friendship (such as Harry Potter's friends), circumstances (such as a class of kids at school), a common interest (such as baby-sitting or playing on a sports team) or a common goal (such as the Animorph friends uniting to save the world from alien invasion). Sometimes one friend will always be the main character (like Harry Potter), but usually each different book in the series will feature one main character from the group. For example, if there are six characters in the group, the first, seventh, thirteenth book and so on will be written from one character's perspective, while the second, eighth, fourteenth book and so on will be written from the perspective of one of the other kids.

Series books are usually plot driven, in that the group of friends are struggling to solve a problem that is similar in all the books. In the Baby-Sitters Club books, for instance, the problem always centers around a situation that arises when the club members are baby-sitting. In the Animorph books, the problem always centers around finding and setting back the efforts of the alien invaders. The main character may have to face a weakness to deal with the problem in that particular book, but that will only be slight character growth, because you always have to leave room for more potential growth in future books.

Read the Pros

1. Read *First Test* in the The Protector of the Small series by Tamora Pierce. In Kel's first year on probation as a page, she is determined to prove that she deserves the right to try for her shield as a female knight. See how Kel confronts her fear of heights, but still has plenty of room for growth in future books in the series.
2. Read several books in either The Baby-Sitters Club series by Ann M. Martin

or the Animorphs series by Katherine Applegate, each with different main characters. See the similarities in each series, along with the differences in narrative voice based on each particular book's main character. See how the main character grows and changes just a little in each book.

Finding out you've got more to say

Once in a while a single novel will be so successful that the writer decides to write a sequel. In this case, your main character will already have experienced his moment of profound growth. You'll have to think about your reason for wanting to write this sequel. If you, your readers and your editor liked a secondary character, then your sequel may feature that kid as the hero. That will give you an opportunity for coming up with a way for this new character to change and grow in his own right.

Your character may have grown more complex as you wrote the book, and even though your novel seems complete, you're left with a sense of unfinished business. You find yourself continuing to think about this character after the first book is done. In this case, you've discovered a character worthy of a sequel because his or her story isn't really over yet.

If everyone liked the plot—for example, an appealing ghost story—then your sequel may follow the same plot line. The main character could meet a different ghost, but under similar circumstances. If he helped a ghost find something the first time, he could help a different ghost in a different way the second time. As you plan the quest, think about a new way for your main character to grow in this novel.

Sequels pose special problems in that you must balance the background information about these characters for old and new readers. If some readers aren't familiar with the first book, you need to put in enough information about the characters to introduce them without boring old readers. Do this by saying it in a different way. The reader might first see the characters from the original book in the middle of an activity or an adventure that reveals necessary background information through what the characters do and say. Come up with new situations and problems, rather than just covering the same territory as the first book, so the sequel stands on its own for the new reader, and the old reader feels that he's having a new experience.

Kids come to a sequel optimistically because they made friends with the characters in the first book. But they often like that first book best because of the joy of discovery—the subsequent books seem less satisfying because they cover the same sort of ground. Keep your sequel fresh by letting your characters take the reader somewhere new. Put the familiar characters in a new setting, or introduce them to a new character. This allows the characters your readers have befriended to develop in new and different ways, and it may even lead you to write more than one sequel.

Read the Pros

1. Read *Ramona the Pest* by Beverly Cleary. See how the author took one character from her successful *Beezus and Ramona* and used her as the basis for a new series.

2. Read *Stinker's Return* by Pamela F. Service. Readers are pleased to see Karen, Jonathan and the alien Stinker again from *Stinker From Space*. See how the author introduces an entirely new type of character in the sequel in Trevor Conway, the has-been movie star. This opens up a whole new set of problems in the sequel, as well as taking Stinker and his human friends to an entirely new setting.

3. Read *The Ghost Wore Gray* by Bruce Coville. Nina and Chris had so much success solving a ghostly mystery in *The Ghost in the Third Row* that the author brings them back for a repeat performance.

TRY IT YOURSELF: SERIES CHARACTERS

1. Look over the stories you've written or planned out. Does one of the secondary characters interest you? Would you like to explore this character on his own? Plan out a story that would feature this secondary character in the main role.

2. Think about the protagonists you've developed. Is there one character you enjoyed writing about and would like to see more of? Plan a new story that develops this character beyond the first story.

3. Take one character from a story you've written (either a main character or a secondary character). Choose one character trait you mentioned, and plan how this trait could lead your character into new problems or different plot directions in a new story.

4. Have you written a story with a situation you and your readers enjoyed? Think about a variation on that situation for a new story, such as:
   ★ a treasure hunt set in a different location searching for a different type of treasure
   ★ a ghost story in which the character meets a different ghost from a different time period
   ★ a club story in which a different member of the club tackles a variation of the club problem, as in the Baby-Sitters Club series
   ★ a school story that features a different member of the class facing a school problem

Furry characters are "people," too

Look at the delighted face of a child curled up with each particular book *The Adventures of Peter Rabbit* or *Winnie-the-Pooh*, and you'll yearn to write talking animal stories. But there seems to be some magic involved in getting these animals to say anything, because editors often warn in their guidelines: "No talking animals!" It's not that editors don't love fuzzy creatures as much as children do. The problem is that many writers take shortcuts in creating animal characters, expecting the animal's cuteness quotient to take the place of character development, and they even write in an arch tone. If you want to write talking-animal stories, develop your animal characters fully.

Just like your human characters, your animal character must face a story problem and struggle to resolve it. This should be a believable problem that a small child can take seriously: making a new friend at school, dealing with a baby brother or sister, giving a grandparent a special gift or tagging after an older sibling. Don't be deceived by the cute exterior of animal characters—just like human characters, your animals need to display genuine emotions. Let the animal express the yearning, humor, misery and triumph of facing real problems to reflect the honest hopes and fears that your readers experience in their own lives.

As you develop appealing animal characters, be sure to have a reason you're writing about a certain type of animal as opposed to a different animal or a person. Your sympathetic wolf might have big teeth but he only sinks them into layer cakes. Your pig eats too much, but he turns up his nose at slops and dines out at his favorite gourmet restaurant. Don't let the characteristics of the real animal influence your fictional character too heavily, however. All wolves aren't necessarily fierce, and pigs don't have to be dirty. It's fine to have your story bear determined to get honey, like a real bear, but let him try genuinely creative ways to get it, the way Pooh decides to roll in the mud then float up on a sky-blue balloon, pretending to be a rain cloud. Kids want to see fun, quirky characters, whether they're human or animal.

Once you've developed a believable character with real qualities that kids will recognize in themselves, give your character a real name. Too often talking animals come into stories with alliterative names like Freddy Fish or even Chip the Chipmunk. These names bore young readers instead of charming them; they're also a sign that authors haven't taken the time to fully develop their characters. What's that fish really like? Joker might be a fun name for a clown fish who takes his species with a grain of salt. If you really like the sound of alliteration, be sure it means something. That talkative chipmunk might be named Chatterbox.

TRY IT YOURSELF: ANIMAL CHARACTERS, PART I

1. Pick a type of animal you find appealing—perhaps a parrot, octopus, cat or hippopotamus. Decide what this animal is like as a character, and give him a fun name that reflects his nature rather than just his species. Give him a story problem and plan out a story that might feature this animal hero.

2. Think about traits associated with certain animals. Use these traits in unexpected ways to involve your anthropomorphized animal character in a story. For example, you might write about a cowardly chicken who is hiding from the fox. He is inspired by the act of hiding in the barn to find a way to outsmart the fox—perhaps luring the hunter inside so the fox falls through a trap door.

3. Select a type of animal you could imagine dressing in human clothes, such as a bear, mouse or elephant. Turn this animal into a character in its own humanlike society to illuminate the human situation for your young readers.

4. Take the same animal you developed in exercise 3. Now let this character interact with a human character. Write several scenes to experiment with different reactions:

   ★ One is delighted to meet the other and completely willing to suspend disbelief. How would the other react?

   ★ One convinces the other to suspend disbelief. How could that be done?

   ★ They might both be afraid of each other when they first meet.

   ★ One might be more frightened of the other. If it's the animal character, what will he or she do to show fear? If it's the human, what would that character do?

   ★ Fear can lead to aggression. How might one of them attack the other? How could they overcome that to make friends?

   ★ The two become friends—then either another animal or another human sees them. What could happen?

Select names for your animals that reflect each character's quirky personality, just the way you would for your human characters.

Animal characters can unleash your readers' imaginations. They allow kids to explore the pains, worries and delights of childhood in a safe fictional world that is less threatening than real life. Animal stories step back just far enough from the real world to give readers the perspective to see their own lives more clearly. Give your talking animals something worth saying, and you'll be able to create believable, endearing animal characters that help small children grow.

Read the Pros

1. Read *Frog and Toad Are Friends* by Arnold Lobel and *Little Bear* by Else Holmelund Minarik. See how these comforting animal characters help small children understand the concepts of friendship and of love between mother and child.
2. Read *Stuart Little* by E.B. White and *The Wind in the Willows* by Kenneth Graham. See how these authors create animals who behave like small people, down to giving them human clothes and actually allowing them to interact with humans and other species on an equal basis.
3. Read *Freddy the Detective* by Walter R. Brooks. See how each animal is a wonderfully developed character with a distinct personality.
4. Read *Redwall* by Brian Jacques. See how the author has created an entire rodent civilization with a full cast of characters who interact as the main mouse character works to achieve his quest against the rats.

Animals who keep quiet

Some animal stories feature realistic animals in their actual environment, as opposed to talking animals. These animal characters behave believably as members of their species. For small children, this can introduce them to the wonders of the animal world by blending in accurate wildlife details about habitat and behavior with an entertaining story. For older readers, this allows writers to show the gulf between the so-called civilized world of people and the so-called wild world of animals.

Stories about realistic animals require research. You're not so much creating a fictional character as you are writing about real animals. If you've got a dog you're especially close to, you might be able to write a strong dog story like *Big Red* by Jim Kjelgaard or *The Call of the Wild* by Jack London. Your writer's imagination provides the plot, and your knowledge of dogs and their behavior provides the realism that will bring the animal character to life for your reader.

You can write a realistic animal story from the point of view of the animal itself, letting it be the main character. To do this you must think like that animal, and see the world from its perspective. A dog might not know what a computer is, for example. He might think of it as a box that hums and whirs and fills with light and pictures, and he might wish

TRY IT YOURSELF: ANIMAL CHARACTERS, PART II

1. Think of a real animal you have contact with—perhaps a pet dog or cat, birds you feed, deer in the nearby woods or geese that use the neighborhood lake as a stop in their migratory pattern. Based on your knowledge of this animal, develop it into a character and decide how you might use it in a story in which it would interact with humans.

2. Do some research on a real animal you've always been interested in, such as a white rhinoceros or a great blue heron. Based on what you discover, plan out a story about this animal set in its natural habitat. Try writing some of this story in the first person, in the animal's own natural voice, as if it were telling the story to other animals who would recognize it easily.

3. Choose a dangerous wild animal, such as a poisonous snake, hungry hawk, hunting cougar or rabid dog. Plan out a story in which this animal is the enemy, and create a kid protagonist who can confront the animal in the wild.

4. Come up with a problem that arises from animal-human interaction, such as a cockroach facing the exterminator or a panda looking out through the bars in a zoo. Write this confrontation from the animal character's perspective.

---

his person would spend more time playing with him and less time sitting in front of the box.

Some realistic animal stories take place solely in the animal's world, without any human characters at all. But most of them feature human characters who befriend, threaten or are threatened by the wildlife around them. In these stories, the animal might be the enemy—a fox mother might attack an isolated human who tries to set up camp in her domain, threatening her babies. Or the kid might be the enemy, capturing a wild animal and bringing it back to "civilization" away from its home. Another option is to let the kid try to tame a wild animal—perhaps the youngster doesn't have human friends and is lonely. The two of them might then be united against a common enemy that threatens either the kid or the animal's habitat.

If you're an animal lover and you feel able to think like an animal, you may enjoy developing animal characters in your stories even more than human characters. Even in writing realistic fiction you'll find you have to anthropomorphize a little. Writers can't be crippled by the fear that real animals wouldn't think exactly that way. In *Watership Down*, for example, Richard Adams has created a very believable rabbit society (more believable than Beatrix Potter's rabbit society in *The Adventures of Peter Rabbit*, for example), but real rabbits probably don't think quite like these fictional rabbits. Because your audience is human, your animals should think in ways that make sense to human readers, at the same time that you're being true to what you know about these real animals.

 Read the Pros

1. Read *Black Beauty* by Anna Sewell. See how the author manages to write in the strong narrative voice of the horse, without letting human assumptions intrude into the horse's perception of the world. Contrast this with the way Walter Farley shows the Black through Alec's eyes in *The Black Stallion*. Both are compelling portraits of believable horses, from entirely different perspectives.
2. Read the Barkley books by Marilyn D. Anderson. Writing from a dog's perspective, the author shows Barkley's adventures believably as he searches cross-country to find his master, Jamie.
3. Read *Rascal* by Sterling North. See how the author shows the delight and frustrations of raising a wild raccoon. This book encourages middle graders to respect the distance between the human and animal worlds.

Aliens and microchips

Some characters come from other worlds. Despite the fact that they may be alien beings or inorganic objects like robots, these characters need to be just as human as the other characters you create. Some writers concentrate entirely on the word "science" in the science-fiction genre, and forgetting that it's really about good fiction—and good fiction is about strong characters. Since you're writing for humans, be careful not to get so hung up on making your characters alien that you overlook their essential humanity. Forget the special effects and the gizmos, and look for ways to make your characters quirky and engaging.

Talking-animal stories allow you to step back from the real world to show small readers concepts they may be more receptive to coming from furry animals than from other children. In a similar way, science fiction allows you to explore potentially disturbing topics in a safer way for older kids. Perhaps one of your characters is an alien who's getting picked on by the human kids at a school on a distant space station. The reader would

TRY IT YOURSELF: ALIEN CHARACTERS

1. Imagine a race from a different planet. Plan out what they would look like and what they would value, based on what their home world is like. Create a character from this race who has a problem that your reader could relate to. Then develop your character. What is it like, and what will it do about this problem?

2. Take some celestial body from astronomy, such as a black hole or a wormhole that can move through time and space, and imagine that it could be a sentient being. Develop it as a character. Use what science knows about it and show how it might have desires and abilities that could interact with humans to help or to hinder.

3. Plan out a robot character. Inside the gears and microchips, give it enough artificial intelligence to think and want. Plan out quirky mannerisms and habits that would make this character both appealing and frustrating to the humans around it.

---

read about him and think about the issues of discrimination—perhaps more open-mindedly than he would if you were writing about racial discrimination in a school that might be right down the block from him.

Develop your alien characters the same way you develop your human characters. Suppose you want to write about a Martian. Remember to avoid simplistic or alliterative names, such as Marty the Martian, for a start. Give him a name that sounds alien, but something that the reader can sound out and pronounce—Zbloorfgtii is too hard for readers to manage, but Zyyrgh would work. Decide what Zyyrgh wants and why, and decide what obstacles he'll run up against in getting it. Plan out what Zyyrgh is afraid of, what he likes to do and what he's looking for in a martian—or human—friend. Also be ready to turn the reader's expectations upside down. If the main character is human and the aliens are supposed to be a terrifying threat to everyone on Earth, perhaps Zyyrgh is no threat to your human hero and may be afraid of the Earthlings himself.

Robots look as if they should be classed with inanimate objects, but in fact, robots can have minds of their own. With the wonders of artificial intelligence, robots can think and reason—at least as far as their programming allows. Some robots can even be designed to reprogram themselves, which means the sky's the limit for what they can come up with, and what trouble they can get into. You might write about Krono VI, an advanced-series robot who's supposed to tutor chemistry in school but has given himself the programming of a poet. What would he end up teaching the kids he's helping? How would they react?

Let your imagination loose in creating science-fiction characters. You might want to write about an entirely alien civilization or about an encounter between humans and aliens. A human kid on a space shuttle might find an alien kid who's a stowaway on the cargo deck, and you could explore the issues of friendship and trust between them. Or a young service robot with flexible programming could decide the kid who lives in his house is a pain and needs reprogramming, and you could explore the issues of expectation and individuality. Make your aliens and robots quirky and human at heart, and your readers will look at the universe in a whole new way.

Read the Pros

1. Read *Under Alien Stars* by Pamela F. Service, which takes place after Earth has been invaded by the alien Tsorians. See how the author develops a compelling alien character in Aryl, who views the humans her father rules as the true aliens. When Aryl and the human boy Jason have to work together to save both races from an even more dangerous alien invasion, both Aryl and Jason find themselves questioning who is truly alien.

2. Read *So You Want to Be a Wizard* by Diane Duane. Phred is a white hole who is accidentally attracted by Nita's and Kit's spell. This alien character proves himself to be poignantly human as he begins by only wanting to deliver a message to the wizards so he can go back home, but ends by going nova to help his friends battle the Lone Power.

3. Read *The A.I. Gang: Robot Trouble* by Bruce Coville. When the gang decides to launch Twerpy, Dr. Weiskopf's singing robot, into space, Twerpy takes on a life of his own.

Breathing life into inanimate characters

Some characters are neither alive nor cognizant without the animation of the reader's imagination. While animals and aliens are at least animate to begin with, some writers like to write about inanimate objects such as pencils, toothbrushes or toys. This genre presents special challenges in convincing the reader to suspend disbelief and accept these objects as believable characters.

Toys are perhaps the easiest way to capture the reader's belief, because most children can imagine that their toys come to life when human backs are turned. In a fantasy you could easily animate a teddy bear or doll and have the reader willingly suspend disbelief. In this case, you would give these characters the same personality attributes you would give your human characters. The main challenge comes when you decide you want human children and toys that have come to life to interact. Since the reader hasn't had his toys run around and talk to him (except in his imagination), he'll be a little startled by this. The best way to persuade the reader to suspend disbelief is to let the human child in the story be startled to have her toys come to life also. Once she accepts the magic of this fantastic occurrence, the reader will accept it, too.

It's harder to believably animate truly inanimate objects such as a toothbrush. Sometimes writers think it's clever to write a story about Toby Toothbrush that teaches readers the importance of brushing their teeth—but kids won't fall for this didactic ploy. They know that Toby is the thinly disguised voice of their dentist or mother, ordering them to brush their teeth whether they want to or not. While Alistair the swimming toothbrush who longs to perform water ballet in the bathtub is immediately more appealing as a character, it's hard to believe that a toothbrush could come to life. How can he swim? He has no legs to kick, no arms to paddle, and he's not flexible enough to swim like an eel. If you decide to use a familiar household object as a character in your story, be sure you have a convincing reason to make it into an animate character, and be sure you can believably get the object to move and take action in the context of your story.

If you can do that, then have fun with your inanimate object character. Make it as quirky and individualistic as the other characters in your fiction. Give it a unique, nonalliterative name, and show its character growth. Whether your character is a child, a white hole, a toy soldier or a vacuum cleaner, stretch your imagination to make his or her (or its!) personality well rounded and unexpected, and show character growth. Your reader will make a friend who will live on long after the story is over.

 **Read the Pros**

1. Read *The Indian in the Cupboard* by Lynne Reid Banks. See how the author turns the toy models into animate characters by allowing Omri to use the cupboard's magic. These characters now display a complex blend of traits and qualities like any human character.

TRY IT YOURSELF: INANIMATE CHARACTERS

1. Take a familiar household object, and think about how you would bring it to life. What goal could it have, or what could it want? Write a scene in which it moves around on its own trying to achieve this.
2. Select a toy and make it come alive. Write a scene describing how it would move and speak. Decide how its voice would sound.
3. Take the inanimate object you brought to life in exercise 1 and plan a scene in which a kid sees it. How will the kid react? How will the object react? Write the scene from the kid's point of view. Then turn it around and write the same scene from the object's point of view.

---

2. Read *Davin* by Dan Gordon and Zaki Gordon. The story-within-a-story technique in this book allows the authors to create a believable fantasy in which a group of toys battle cats, pirates and other toys to find a magical teddy bear who holds the power to save a sick child.
3. Read *The Brave Little Toaster* by Thomas M. Disch. See how the author gives the toaster and his fellow appliances quirky personalities so that their humanity is limited only by their parts and wiring as they work together to find the boy who owned them.

KEEPING GROWN-UPS IN THEIR PLACE
Adult Characters

Kids may learn classroom lessons from adult teachers, but they learn life lessons from experience, not from grown-ups telling them what to do. Fiction is an ideal way for a reader to learn life lessons as the story character experiences them, because the reader identifies with this character—it's as if he's learning the lesson, too. While one form of experience is to observe grown-ups as role models (both positive and negative), neither the story character nor the reader will listen if an adult steps in and tries to tell the kids what to do.

But adults are a constant part of a kid's life—parents, grandparents, teachers, ministers, coaches, the ice-cream truck driver on his block, the store owner who suspects him of shoplifting, the neighbor who expects him to shovel her walk for free. Just the way you find child characters all around you and in your memories, you'll find adult characters in your friends, neighbors and memories of the adults you grew up with. These characters have their places in the stories you write, but you can't let them take over, no matter how hard they may try. Instead, use your adult characters to intensify the plot by making them believable and fallible.

Imperfect adults

Adults in your stories need to be well-rounded characters, just like the kids. They must be a mixture of insight and blindness, and good and

163

evil. As characters, they will become more believable, and your story will become more complex and interesting for the reader, if you allow them to make mistakes or even become the enemy. Suppose Santiago is having difficulties fitting in at a new school. A teacher who mispronounces his name, gets embarrassed over it, makes a snide joke to cover it, and then feels uncomfortable about Santiago and picks on him in class will worsen the story problem considerably. That teacher will also be more recognizable to the reader than a saccharine sweet teacher who goes overboard in welcoming Santiago into the classroom and does everything to smooth his way in adapting to his new school.

Even more believable would be a teacher who has her own problems. Perhaps Mrs. Woodrow is getting a divorce, and her son wants to live with his father. She's angry and hurting that morning when she comes to class and stumbles over Santiago's name, and the incident becomes mixed up with her other problems in her mind, so she is unable to come right out and apologize to him. She finds herself calling on him when she sees he's not paying attention or singling him out when a bunch of students are making noise. Santiago feels (justifiably!) picked on, and Mrs. Woodrow becomes increasingly uncomfortable around him. The reader wouldn't know all the background about the teacher since Santiago would be the viewpoint character, unless he overhears her talking to another teacher about her problems. But it would become clear that she's more than a cardboard "teacher" character in the story. And, because she's struggling to resolve her own problems just as Santiago is struggling to resolve his, she might find a way to make it up to him at a critical moment in your plot—believably helping him without wresting control of the story from him.

Also, adult characters may simply be wrong. When Mrs. Woodrow sees Santiago in the hallway, arguing with two of her best students, she assumes it's Santiago's fault since he's the new kid. Perhaps she's had trouble with a Hispanic student in the past and assumes that all Hispanic kids will be trouble. She fails to see Santiago as an individual and doesn't stop to find out what really happened.

And some adult characters may ultimately be the enemy. While most fiction for small children shows adults in a positive light, fiction for adolescents takes into account that adults aren't always trustworthy. A parent may tell his kids he cheats on his taxes, as if it's something to be proud of. A neighbor might abuse his wife, and all the neighborhood kids see her with bruises.

Just as you give your heroes flaws and your villains positive qualities, look for ways to give your adult characters a mixture of weak-

TRY IT YOURSELF: ADULT CHARACTERS, PART I

1. Develop a parent character, either a mother or father. Decide whether that character wanted to be a parent and why. What personality characteristics can you give this character? Balance strengths and weaknesses as you develop this parent's interaction with the child main character.

2. Create a teacher character. Decide whether this teacher likes to teach (and why) or whether it's only a job. Now decide whether this character is a good teacher or not. Write a scene in class that shows this teacher trying to deal with his or her students.

3. Create an adult villain. This character could be a parent, teacher or neighbor. Decide what this character is doing to the main character, and write a scene early in the story that shows the adult in a position of power over the kid. Now write a confrontation scene late in the story when the kid takes control.

---

nesses and strengths so that readers will accept grown-ups as part of the story instead of the voice of authority.

Read the Pros

1. Read *A Solitary Blue* by Cynthia Voigt. See how the author contrasts two dysfunctional parents in Melodie and the Professor to create two wholly believable adult characters.

2. Read *You Can Call Me Worm* by Dan Haas. As Worm and Todd hike through the woods to find their father after their parents' separation, they discuss him. See how the author develops him through their conversations as a believable, sympathetic parent before revealing that he's manic-depressive.

3. Read *Shiloh* by Phyllis Reynolds Naylor. See how the author creates a dangerous villain in Judd Travers. Travers becomes more believable as Marty grudgingly discovers a few admirable qualities in him. Then the author gives Travers some justification for his meanness in his unhappy childhood.

Where did they get all the answers?

Kids have nothing against reading about adults in secondary roles, as long as they don't take over the story and tell everyone what to do. When you're tempted to write about a grown-up who knows everything, stop and ask yourself how that adult got so smart. When Mrs. Woodrow is unfair to Santiago, Mr. Akbar, the P.E. teacher, is tempted to explain that he understands. He wants to urge Santiago to just go on being himself, and the teacher will realize in time that he's a good kid, the same way that she'll sooner or later figure out that her "best" students are the real troublemakers. But Mr. Akbar wasn't born knowing that— how did he learn it? Very possibly he had to deal with his own version of Mrs. Woodrow when he was growing up, and he learned that he had to just wait until the teacher saw his real worth, or find some other way to show her.

Perhaps his way came through sports, which is why he teaches P.E. now. Mr. Akbar shouldn't preach at Santiago that a sport will put him in a better position to change Mrs. Woodrow's mind, but he might encourage the boy to try a sport. Maybe Santiago will shine at track, and as he grows more confident and gains the respect of some of the other students, he'll be able to show Mrs. Woodrow that she was wrong about him. Santiago has made the effort, and Mr. Akbar has served as a mentor and a friend, without taking over the story.

Kids often have adults as friends, so long as the adult doesn't make all the decisions. And they look for mentors in the older kids and the adults around them. While it can be hard for a kid to be friends with a parent, you can develop other family members who can relate to your young characters on a more equitable basis. It helps if these adults aren't currently raising children of their own, and therefore don't feel the need to "parent" all the time. A childless aunt or uncle or a grandparent can be an important character in your book.

In *The Ghost Cadet*, Benjy and his sister meet their grandmother for the first time when they're sent to spend spring vacation with her in Virginia. Shy and troubled, Benjy doesn't expect her to like him, but she accepts him as he is and the two of them form a tight bond by the end of the book. She's not a typical doting granny, however. Since she feels distant from the rest of her family, she prefers to be called Miss Leota instead of Grandmother. Rather than bake, she has a store-bought cake to welcome them. But she has a number of attitudes that make Benjy feel comfortable with her right away. She doesn't think a person should be judged by his or her age, but by what he or she can accomplish. From Miss Leota's perspective, that means she resents being forced to retire from her teaching job because of her age. But she extends this attitude to Benjy, treating him as an equal when she feels he acts like one—and treating his older sister like a small brat when she acts like one, much to Benjy's delight. Miss Leota also values aspects of Benjy's character

TRY IT YOURSELF: ADULT CHARACTERS, PART II

1. Write a character sketch of a childless relative who comes to visit after a long absence or even for the first time in your character's memory. Show what qualities will make this adult character interesting to the youngster, and lay the foundation for their becoming friends.

2. Write a conversation between a youngster and an adult he or she sees everyday, such as the seller in a newsstand, the cashier at the local McDonald's or the bus driver. Experiment with the different attitudes, such as:

   ★ The adult may be in a hurry to get somewhere and might not be interested in talking to the kid. How does the youngster win the adult over?

   ★ The adult may be afraid of getting into trouble talking to a strange kid. How might the youngster make friends?

   ★ Think of something they might appear to have in common that will get them talking. Perhaps the adult is reading a children's book for an adult education class (or for personal pleasure!), or perhaps the adult is wearing a sweater featuring a children's character such as the Cat in the Hat.

   ★ Both the adult and the youngster may be shy. How do they overcome it to talk to each other?

3. Choose an adult in a position to be influential in a kid's life, such as a teacher, coach or even a friend's parent. Write a character sketch that shows what it is about that adult your young character might admire—perhaps a friend's parent who fought in the Gulf War and likes to tell exciting stories, or a teacher the kid sees singing and dancing at the community theater tryouts.

---

that most people do not, such as his bookishness and his privacy. She's a stern disciplinarian, but doesn't question Benjy about his activities once she makes up her mind that he's responsible.

To develop a believable adult character who can interact with your youngsters, show how a grown-up can treat a child with respect, acknowledging his abilities and his potential, and giving him room to grow into it rather than pushing him into it. These adults offer guidance not with lectures, but through the example of their behavior and through the close friendship they can form with the young people who look up to them. They can be teachers, coaches, scout leaders, neighbors or even someone the youngster doesn't know well, such as the lawn man or the librarian. Kids often hang around adults they admire and strike up unexpected friendships, discovering things about themselves and about the adults along the way. So be prepared to make room for this type of adult in your character cast. And sometimes the best way to write about adults that kids look up to is to profile real adult role models in nonfiction, as you'll see in Part IV.

Read the Pros

1. Read *The True Confessions of Charlotte Doyle* by Avi. The author gives Charlotte an unexpected friend in Zachariah and develops their relationship as it evolves through suspicion, distrust, grief, friendship and mentoring.

2. Read *The Village by the Sea* by Paula Fox. See how Emma grows to understand Aunt Bea's peculiar behavior after the miniature seaside village that Emma has made with a friend is destroyed.

Quirky adults kids will love

The adult character must transcend the banal, whether the character is a friend and a mentor, a parent or a character who appears regularly but doesn't profoundly influence the way the protagonist resolves the story situation. Throw out the stereotypes—Mom doesn't stay home cleaning and cooking anymore, Dad doesn't leave all the domestic work to Mom, Granny doesn't knit and Grandad doesn't nap in his garden. Of course your characters may do these things part of the time, but their defining characteristics should transcend these outdated impressions.

Perhaps Mom loves cars. She might work on an assembly production line and spend her evenings and weekends fixing up a classic Corvette with Dad. Dad might work at home—he could be an artist, a writer, a caterer. Or he could be a musician who works weekend nights. On weekdays, he carpools the kids and fixes supper. Grandparents may be retired, but that doesn't mean they sit around watching television, knitting and crocheting, or going fishing. Maybe Grandma got hooked on computers and she's launched her own shareware company. It takes all her free time to handle orders, keep her Web page updated and write new programs. She doesn't knit sweaters for her grandkids, but she writes terrific personalized game programs for them. Grandpa has gotten exercise-conscious in his old age. He's started taking tennis lessons and is training for a senior tennis competition.

TRY IT YOURSELF: QUIRKY ADULTS

1. Make notes in your character journal for nontraditional parents. Perhaps both work at home and split the domestic chores. Perhaps neither has time for domestic chores, and they eat a lot of frozen dinners, takeout and delivery, while dust bunnies frolic under the furniture. Write a paragraph in the voice of one of their kids that expresses their feelings about their parents.

2. Write a character sketch of a grandmother who adores her grandchildren but shows it in unconventional ways. Instead of baking cookies and knitting booties, for example, she might take them to the mall and beat them at video games, or make them dinosaur planters for their bedrooms in her pottery class. Be respectful of her age, but let her be eccentric. Decide how her quirky traits could enhance a story that featured her.

3. Plan out an adult character in a specific role (coach, teacher, housekeeper, neighbor):

   ★ First make a list of stereotypical comments about that role. Choose only one or two comments from that list.

   ★ Now make a list of atypical characteristics you might assign to this character. Select several, even if they don't seem to make sense.

   ★ Write a character sketch that combines those few stereotypical characteristics and the atypical personality traits to create a well-rounded character.

As soon as you make your adult family members more quirky, you make them more interesting for the reader. Use the same techniques to develop other adults in your stories. Let the football coach rescue stray cats and keep them while he's trying to find homes for them. Give that math teacher a sense of humor that brings word problems to life. Use gay and lesbian characters as positive role models instead of stereotypes, and don't use their orientation as their primary characteristic. A gay neighbor doesn't have to have perfectly tended flower beds—his hobby might be carving wooden furniture and his workshop could be chaotic. Kids need to be introduced to the diversity of human experience in the characters they meet on the page to prepare them for the multitude of characters they'll meet in real life.

Read the Pros

1. Read *Holes* by Louis Sachar. See how the author creates a comic adult villain in the Warden of Camp Green Lake and an unconventional school teacher in Kissing Kate Barlow.

2. Read *Split Just Right* by Adele Griffin. See how the author surrounds Dandelion (Danny) with a whole cast of quirky adults, including her actress mother who lives in a world of half-truths, and their gay neighbor, Gary, a computer software analyst who makes up nicknames for Danny and lets her vent about her problems while he mourns his partner, dead from AIDS.

3. Read *A View From Saturday* by E.L. Konigsburg. See how the author creates a strong character in Mrs. Olinski, a paraplegic teacher who draws her students together for the Academic Team, without letting her take control of them as they sort out their relationships and their problems, and discover their special strengths. Konigsburg is especially good at crafting unique, appealing adult characters. Also look at the title character in *From the Mixed-Up Files of Mrs. Basil E. Frankweiler* and the detective's sidekick in *The Dragon in the Ghetto Caper.*

Getting adults out of the way

Sometimes even the best adult characters have to be taken out of a story to let the main character come into his own. When Ian is tracking a ghost, for example, he knows his parents wouldn't let him go to the graveyard late at night, so they need to believably disappear. In Victorian novels, the adults used to be sent to India, leaving the children on their own in a boarding school or with distant relatives who didn't watch them too closely. In modern times, the world has shrunk, and unless you're writing science fiction and the adults can be sent to a space station on Neptune while their children remain on Earth, writers need to find more creative ways of getting rid of the grown-ups.

Single-parent families can be one way to take care of the adults and simultaneously deepen the character's internal problems. If Ian's mother is out of the picture and his father works long hours, perhaps he would find Dad asleep in front of the television and be able to creep out on his own. Or if Dad has an out-of-town business trip and leaves Ian with friends or a grandparent, he might find himself less closely supervised than usual and be able to slip out to chase after that ghost. But the lack of supervision could translate into lack of concern to Ian—perhaps he's trying to solve the mystery of the ghost to get his father's attention.

TRY IT YOURSELF: GETTING ADULTS OUT OF THE WAY

1. Brainstorm a list of activities that might get a parent out of the house at a crucial time for your character. Select one and decide how your character will use it to his or her advantage. Also decide how he feels about it. Is he delighted that Mom plays bridge four times a week, or is he lonely because Mom's too busy to listen to him talk about his day at school?

2. Make a list of excuses kids could use to get out of the house on their own. Keep this list in your character journal so you can refer to it next time you're stuck with stay-at-home parents and a character who needs some freedom. Work out what the consequences will be once the parents realize the kids snuck out.

3. Brainstorm problems a parent might have that prevent him or her from paying attention to a child. Decide how a kid might cope with one of these problems. You could use this situation as the basis for a story. Or you could use these problems to add depth to a story you've been working on that has seemed too simple and straightforward.

Sometimes clever kids can manipulate the adults in their lives to look the other way. If Ian's parents are divorced instead, and they share custody, he could play them against each other, so that each of them think he's with the other the night he goes ghost hunting. Ian might manage this even if he has a full complement of parents. He could distract them by focusing attention on a sibling who's in trouble, or he could tell them he's doing a school project at a friend's house and detour to the haunted graveyard after a cursory meeting with his friend. However, your character shouldn't lie to adults or break rules with impunity. Having your character do illegal or dangerous things without suffering any consequences sets a bad example for your reader. Let the character realize that he shouldn't be lying or sneaking out, but that he feels he's forced into taking such an action because of the imperative nature of the story situation.

Parents may also have their own problems that distract them from their kids. If Ian's parents are worried about their own aging parents, for example, they might pay less attention to Ian (who seems to be fine) than they pay to their parents, who seem to be the ones suddenly needing the parenting. Problems at work could make Ian's father moody, so that Ian can slip out when he's supposed to be doing his homework. Or a parent could be unwell or unbalanced mentally, and be unable to care for his or her children any longer. Showing these problems from the child character's perspective both builds sympathy for the adult character and gets him out of the way so that Ian (and the reader) can concentrate on the story problem in peace.

Read the Pros

1. Read *The Lion, the Witch and the Wardrobe* by C.S. Lewis. This is a classic example of how children are separated from their parents (in this case because of the World War II bombing of London) and sent to live with strangers. The Professor's distance from them makes Lucy's discovery of Narnia possible. But the Professor becomes a more intriguing character when the children realize that Lucy's not the only one who believes in this magical world—the Professor does also.

2. Read *Ice* by Phyllis Reynolds Naylor. See how the author uses an ice storm to isolate Chrissa, who's baby-sitting for two small children. Their mother can't get home on the icy roads, but a suspicions stranger appears at the front door, forcing Chrissa to take action to protect the children.

3. Read *Homecoming* by Cynthia Voigt. The mother abandons her children because of her inability to care for them. Yet she remains a sympathetic character through the children's memories of her and their anticipation of seeing her again as they make their journey on their own to their grandmother's home.

Childlike adults

Some stories that children love are entirely about adults. This seems to be a contradiction. How can a child reader identify with an adult character? Particularly in picture books, the protagonist can be an adult who thinks and behaves very much like a child. A young reader who sees adults all around and imagines what it would be like to be grown-up will identify with this childlike adult character. These children will be eager to see how the character deals with story situations as both an assurance that adults are not perfect and as a guide to how they can grow up themselves.

In childlike adults, the dominant characteristic is the one that reflects their childlike quality. The reader doesn't need to know a great deal of background information about the character—if Mr. Rotweiller is grouchy, it's not important to know that he was impatient as a child or that he got good grades in high school. The here and now matters, not the past. It's important that Mr. Rotweiller is grouchy this morning and every morning because his oatmeal is too cold and his orange juice is too warm, and he's grouchy as he walks to work because children zip past him on skateboards munching pop tarts and dropping crumbs. He's grouchy at work because his desk chair is too hard and his computer screen is too bright. He's grouchy walking home because the wind is too strong or the rain is too hard or the fog is too thick or the sun is too hot. Whatever happens, Mr. Rotweiller is grouchy. A character like this doesn't have to be well rounded to become endearing. Like all main characters, however, he has to change. Mr. Rotweiller has to find a way to be happy—or, at least, less grouchy.

Perhaps one day he oversleeps and is very grouchy, so he decides to skip his oatmeal and just drink his orange juice. On the way to work he unexpectedly jumps out of the way of one of the skateboarding kids and snatches his pop tart. He actually smiles at how sweet it tastes, and the kid grins back and waves as he whizzes past to school. As Mr. Rotweiller tries new and different things all day, he becomes less and less grouchy, suggesting to the reader that he might try some new things himself if he's feeling grumpy at life.

Could this story be written about a grouchy child instead of grouchy Mr. Rotweiller? Certainly. Like talking animals, however, a childlike adult gives the reader a little space to see himself more clearly. It can be easier to laugh at the mistakes of a grown-up and see how he should change than it is to look at another child just like yourself and accept that he, like you, should behave differently. Sometimes a child character can help a childlike adult see how to change and grow, or sometimes the childlike adult relies on inner strengths to find the answer. Either way, this character can become someone like an eccentric uncle or aunt that the reader giggles at and learns from along the road to self-discovery.

 Read the Pros

1. Read *Mr. Popper's Penguins* by Richard and Florence Atwater. See how Mr. Popper, with his enthusiasm for explorers and his delight at the penguin Admiral Drake sends him, reflects a childlike sweetness and imagination that appeals to young readers.

2. Read *Silk Peony, Parade Dragon* by Elizabeth Steckman. In this unique telling of a Chinese legend, Mrs. Ming has a dragon farm. When the mandarin decides to take advantage of Mrs. Ming and take one of her dragons for the New Year's Day parade, the story becomes one any child will recognize: the clever, honest Mrs. Ming triumphs over the dishonest bully.

TRY IT YOURSELF: CHILDLIKE ADULTS

1. Choose a childlike quality to be the basis of your adult character, such as imagination, enthusiasm, wonder, innocence, shyness or timidity. List ways that this quality could manifest itself in the common activities of an adult's life that a child reader would recognize. Plan out how this character will deal with a story problem in a way that allows him to grow in ways a child might also grow.

2. Create a childlike adult character who is helped to deal with his problem by making friends with a real child character. Experiment with making the child seem more mature than the adult in the context of the story.

3. Think of something that you've done as an adult that would interest kids, such as exploring castle ruins or getting mistakenly locked inside an office building or a school building after closing. Create a childlike adult character who does this, and use the situation as the basis for a story.

PART IV
Bringing Nonfiction to Life

CHARACTERS FROM LIFE
Real-Life Kids

Creating colorful characters isn't just for fiction. A lot of nonfiction centers around real people, and the same techniques of observation and description that bring characters to life in your stories can help you introduce these real people to young readers. Some nonfiction book series feature high-profile kids and teens such as TV or movie stars, athletes or music sensations, and many magazines are hungry for articles about real kids doing something special. Especially if you find yourself having problems planning out story problems and resolutions, you may find you prefer to put your character writing to work profiling these real-life youngsters.

Tracking down inspiring subjects

To sell a book on a high-profile kid you need to be sure you can reach your subject or the star's family and co-workers to get insider insights. But you can start writing profiles for magazines by finding good subjects much closer to home. You'll be surprised how many interesting kids there are around you. Start by volunteering at your local school. Find out who has recently won special awards or academic contests. For example, is the fifth-grade spelling champion dyslexic? How did she overcome her problem to spell so well? Kids all over the country will want to know— and you've just found a subject for a magazine article.

Talk to the teachers and youth group leaders at your church or synagogue. If a particular youngster or group of kids has won a service award or come up with a unique project that helped someone, you'll have another great subject. Volunteer at your local Boys Club, Girls Club or 4-H club. See if the kids have thought of an unusual community project on their own, such as bagging leaves for elderly home-owners or donating extra livestock to feed the town homeless during the holidays. Coach a sports team or become a team booster. See how the kids work together. Does one help another practice, unasked? Or perhaps one of them has come up with an unexpected way of involving community kids in the sport. Kids helping each other or giving of themselves to help other people can be an inspiration to young readers everywhere.

You can also find inspirational kids by reading your local newspaper, watching the local news on television or listening to the local radio station. Do you have a young pianist who has gone on to try out in a national youth orchestra or a young artist whose work is displayed in a gallery in the state capital? People in your community may already know about this youngster, but you can introduce your local celebrity to a wider readership.

Use these same techniques to find out about kids in other places. Do you have family or friends in another town? Find out about any kids who are doing something special there, and plan to get in touch with them next time you visit. Perhaps a youngster has made the news because she reacted in a crisis, calling 911 and handling things until the adults arrived. Or perhaps a youngster has been in danger and coped with courage and determination, survived a terrible illness through faith or saved another child when both were stranded. Kids like this will make wonderful subjects for profiles that will inspire your readers.

Before you leave for vacation, see if your library has newspapers from the place where you're going. If you see a youngster mentioned in the paper for doing something special, call ahead and see if you can arrange to meet him and interview him. Even if you haven't done any advance planning to contact young celebrities, pick up local newspapers while you travel and listen to the local radio station. Be flexible—perhaps you can schedule an interview while you're in town.

Interviewing young heroes

Have fun while you interview kids. The more relaxed you are and the more you enjoy the interview, the more your subject will relax and open up. If you're too adult and overbearing, you'll end up with mumbles, grunts and "yeah" or "uh-uh" or a reluctant "I guess so," instead of the quotes that will bring the youngster's personality to life for the reader. Your first step is to get permission to interview the kid alone. Meet the parents to introduce yourself and explain that you want to write an article about their child. Once you've won over the parents, ask them to let you and the child talk alone.

This will give you a better interview for two reasons. First, parents will prompt answers that may not be what the youngster really wants to say. Their presence can also inhibit the kid's frankness. Even more important, however, adults tend to talk *to* adults and *about* kids, so if the parents participate in the interview you'll find yourself talking to them over your subject's head. You can interview the parents afterward to confirm facts (kids may exaggerate sometimes) and get their take on their own child's success to round out your impression, but first concentrate on the youngster.

Take some time to make friends with the kid first. Get down on his level—literally. You may be taller, so try not to tower over him. Sit down to get closer to his height. Let him inspect your tape recorder and camera, because if you don't he'll be more interested in your gadgets (which may be strange and new to him) than he is in talking about what he's done (which is old news for him). As soon as he feels comfortable with you, start asking questions so that the interview doesn't outlast his attention span. Be honestly interested in his answers—remember, he's the expert here; that's why you wanted to interview him. If possible, get him to show you what he can do.

For example, suppose you're interviewing Geoff, a kid who organized a petition to save the town park from being turned into a parking lot. First find out how he got the idea and how he persuaded his friends to join him. Have Geoff demonstrate what he'd say to grown-ups when he asked them to sign his petition. Then ask him to share some of his best experiences with you. What reactions did he get from people? What was the most discouraging thing someone said to him? Find out if he ever gave up and what kept him going. Draw him out by asking him open-ended questions, such as, "What didn't you like about it?" You'll find out more that way than you would by asking "yes" or "no" questions such as "Did you like it?"

Even if you use a tape recorder (be sure to test it first to make sure it's recording clearly), also be sure to take notes. Use the observation techniques from chapter 3 to pay attention to how your subject acts. You'll make Geoff seem more alive on the page and more interesting to your reader if you write:

Geoff held out the clipboard politely, with a pen clipped to the petition, ready for signing. The businesslike appearance of his petition was at odds with his faded Star Wars T-shirt and cutoffs. But his shining brown eyes and hopeful smile were as convincing as his argument. "Wouldn't you rather know your kids were playing in the park than hanging out in the mall?" he asked. Nearly every voter Geoff asked said yes. But not all of them.

He frowned at the memory, his petition dropping to his side. "It really made me mad when people said they didn't have kids," he said, "so they didn't see why they should sign the petition." Then he brightened. "But I didn't give up. I asked them if they could remember sitting in the park when they were kids. And wouldn't they have a better time sitting there again than driving for an hour to get out of town." Geoff grinned, showing the chipped front tooth he got playing football. "That got most of them."

You just can't show the reader what Geoff's like in quite the same way by writing:

Geoff's preparation and enthusiasm paid off in hundreds of signatures on his petition.

Show your subject, as well as what he's achieved, so that the reader feels he knows him and longs to be like him by the time he's finished reading your profile. Photographs will help make your subject seem real, but a still photograph can't bring a person to life on the page the way the right words can.

Read the Pros

1. Read *American Girl* magazine. See how the Girls Express section features profiles of girls who are active in sports or the arts, or who participate in interesting cultural activities or hobbies.
2. Read *Guideposts for Kids* and *Guideposts for Teens* magazines, and see how they feature profiles of kids and teens who have made a difference in their communities.
3. Read *New Moon* magazine, and see how the writers profile interesting girls who are active in ways that promote social issues, the arts and the world around them. Contrast these articles with interviews in *Girls' Life* magazine, in which the writers profile girls who are active in sports, entertainment and popular culture.

An interview questionnaire

First get your subject's name (check the spelling) and age. Be sure to get an address and phone number so you can send a copy of the published profile. Then segue smoothly into the interview itself by congratulating your subject on this accomplishment, and start asking questions.

1. Tell me a little bit about what you do.
2. When did you start? Was it your idea, a friend's or your parents'?
3. Did you like doing it at first, or did it get better after a while?
4. What do you like about doing this?
5. How hard is it to do? How long does it take? How much time do you have to spend preparing or practicing?
6. Does the time and effort you put into this cause you any problems with your friends, or do they understand or even help you?
7. Tell me about one time you can remember that made you feel great. What was so special about it?
8. Tell me about one time you can remember that was a disaster. What happened? Did you feel like giving up? Why didn't you?
9. What tips can you give other kids who might want to try something similar?
10. What do you want to do next? Do you want to keep doing this (if it's an activity) or something similar, or do you want to try something new?

Pulling the interview together

You've observed your subject and gotten lots of good quotes and photographs. The youngster you interviewed is vivid in your mind. Now you need to make this kid just as vivid for the reader. To do this you must decide what your profile is really about. Do you want to inspire the reader to start a petition in his own community, like Geoff? Probably not, unless you've found a publication that targets young political activists. To reach most readers in general-interest magazines, look for the main quality that allowed Geoff to succeed with his petition. This might be determination, love of nature or even concern for his little sister who would have no place to play if the park were paved.

To get to the heart of your subject, you need to understand his motivation and where he gets his inner strength to persevere. A young reader might not be interested in getting signatures on a petition, but he could be inspired to find the inner determination to speak out for what he believes. Perhaps after reading about how Geoff changed his town, the reader might decide to stand up for some changes he'd like to see in his school.

Look for a universal positive quality that could inspire all readers.

Depending on your subject, this quality could be courage, faith, determination love of family, acceptance of responsibility for someone else or the ability to overcome adversity. You won't know for sure until you actually talk to the youngster and see why he did what he did and what it cost him to do it. Once you identify this quality, however, you need to focus your profile to bring it out. Select specific quotes and specific incidents that illustrate this quality for your reader. For instance, to show Geoff's determination, you would concentrate on incidents where he struggled to convince someone, rather than his getting the signatures of the ten Greenpeace members in town.

This means you'll have to leave out some of the things you learn in your interview, rather than sharing every aspect of your subject's life with your reader—just the way you need to leave out some of the baggage your characters carry with them when you craft fiction.

Special skills for special markets

Sometimes you actually do want to inspire the reader to learn exactly what your subject has managed to do so well. For special-interest markets, your profile can offer the reader how-to tips from other kids who have become experts at what they do. For example, a magazine that focuses on sports for girls would love an article about a successful gymnast or diver with Olympic aspirations, especially if the article offered specific tips to improve the reader's style or set up a workable practice regimen. An equestrian magazine for kids would be a great market for an article about a young rider who's trained a winning show horse. This article would include the youngster's recommendations to readers on what to look for in selecting a horse with show potential and how to bring out that potential even in less likely horses. For a general-interest magazine, you'd focus on the inner quality that this youngster exemplifies, that readers could find within themselves even if they had no personal interest in trying gymnastics, diving or riding.

To write this sort of article, prepare specific how-to questions for your interview. Ask the youngster how she's achieved what she's done, and use her experiences as a basis for your own how-to tips for readers. Then ask the youngster what advice she'd give kids who were interested in doing what she had done.

Often you can get two different articles out of the same interview. For example, you could write one article for a general-interest magazine that shows the youngster's inner qualities. Then you could write a separate article for a special-interest magazine that offers practical instructions to help readers see how to enjoy the kind of success this youngster has achieved.

TRY IT YOURSELF: CHARACTERS FROM REAL LIFE

1. Read the community news pages in your newspaper. Find an article about a kid who's done something special. Based on the information in the newspaper, plan how you would interview that particular youngster for an article for kids.

2. Talk with a youngster you know—your own child, a student or a neighbor's child—about something interesting he or she has done. Ask yourself what a reader could get out of this youngster's experience. Select about three things your young subject shared with you that would best support the point you want to make. Plan out how you would write an article about this youngster.

3. Talk to a youngster who is good at a particular sport or activity. Find out what tips this youngster could offer other kids. Plan out a how-to article on this subject for a special-interest magazine that focuses on this sport or activity. Show how your subject has done it and what readers could learn from the way this kid has succeeded.

Read the Pros

1. Read *American Cheerleader* magazine. See how the writers profile successful cheerleaders and offer tips on training, fashion and beauty for adolescents and young teens.

2. Read *Stable Kids* magazine. Here, the writers profile young riders and their horses to give readers practical tips on riding and caring for their horses.

3. Read *International Gymnast* magazine. See how the editors publish profiles of young gymnasts with tips on technique, nutrition and competition.

GROWN-UPS KIDS WOULD LOVE TO MEET
Adult Role Models

While kids rarely pay attention to words of wisdom from adults in fiction, they're fascinated by real-life adults who are doing something they dream of doing themselves. Just as you can profile kids who are doing something unique and fascinating, you can also profile intriguing adults. In writing informational nonfiction, you can also turn to adult experts to give you lively quotations, share personal anecdotes and give readers insight into a subject that you can't get from printed or Internet sources. Whether you're introducing your reader to a fascinating adult role model or enhancing a nonfiction manuscript with adult expertise, the key to making the most of these grown-ups is to use vivid writing to bring them to life on the page.

Living the dream

Kids dream of being astronauts, football stars, actors, paleontologists, writers and firemen. Profiling a star athlete or a successful scientist or artist could impress kids that someone has actually done what they dream about, and perhaps inspire the reader to try for it also. You can find subjects for profiles close to home, or get in touch through the telephone or the Internet:

★ If you live near a college or university, you might find interesting subjects among the teaching staff. A large university that has a strong sports program might have athletes who already have name recognition among kids.

★ A visiting celebrity might agree to give you some time in between other commitments.

★ A local artist or writer might agree to an interview.

★ Watch for upcoming events at your library and college, and read the paper for announcements of signings at bookstores. When you find out that someone's coming who you'd like to interview, contact him or her in advance to set up an appointment. Find out who organized their visit locally and ask them who to call or E-mail to arrange this.

★ If you'll be traveling, do some research on the place you'll be visiting to see if any interesting subjects live there. Write or E-mail them in advance to introduce yourself and ask whether you can schedule an interview.

While famous adults are often standoffish if they feel someone is star struck or selfishly hogging their time, they'll often be quite welcoming to a writer who wants to profile them for young readers.

To make these people appeal to your readers, focus on what they have achieved and on interesting anecdotes from their childhood that set up their achievements. Do some advance research to get an idea of what your subject has accomplished, what awards he or she has won and what achievements have garnered the most recognition. You don't want to waste time during the interview going over basics. For authors, read one or two of their books. For scientists, be at least somewhat familiar with their scientific discipline. For musicians, listen to a performance recording and read reviews. Have a working knowledge of the topic and the terminology in advance, so you'll understand what your subject is talking about. Once you've scheduled the appointment, ask your subject or the secretary if you could have a media packet or bio, which gives you the basic facts and clarifies spelling and dates. Most famous people prepare these in advance.

Get to know your subject

Armed with that basic knowledge, get ready to enjoy the interview. Just as you do when you interview kids, you want to strike up a friendship so that your subject will open up to you. Unlike kids, however, you don't do this by getting down with them and letting your adult subject play with your tape recorder. Instead, try to earn the trust of your subjects by establishing your genuine interest in them and your familiarity with their accomplishments. Make a human connection with them by showing you understand and appreciate what they do—a specialist in a technical field, especially, often can't talk to people. A paleontologist may be a genius at spotting fragments of dinosaur eggshells, and a physicist may be able to tie new knots in string theory. When they go to a family reunion or a neighborhood party, however, they can't tell people what they do without having the listener make excuses to get away. Think how much you love to talk about writing—and how few people understand or even care about what you have to say. Like you, this specialist has only a handful of friends in the world who care about what he or she does. If you can show your fascination and your understanding, you'll make your subject eager to open up to you.

After you make friends with your subject, you want to get him talking to capture the flavor of his natural voice. Prepare a number of questions in advance, to draw your subject out, such as asking when and how she became interested in her career, what positive influences had an impact on her, what negative influences she overcame, what she's most proud of in her work, what she's most ashamed of or most regrets and what she aspires to in the future. You're looking for a quality that this subject exemplifies that you can use as the focus of your profile. Sometimes you'll know what this quality is before you start, and sometimes you'll discover it as the interview proceeds. Stay flexible while you're asking the questions. Your subject may be telling you about getting grant funding for a fossil dig and make a side comment about the fun he had talking long cross-country walks as a kid and seeing pieces of dinosaur eggshell sticking up out of the dirt. Funding isn't really the heart of his work—it's his delight at discovering the fossils that tell a tale.

Find a focus

Once you zero in on your focus, try to find about three examples from your subject's life that show the development of this quality. One of these examples should come from the subject's youth if possible—either from his childhood or when he was just starting out. For example, when I wrote "Roy Chapman Andrews and the Secret of the Gobi Desert" for *Highlights for Children*, my focus was the subject's vision and determination. He saw what could be done, and he did it—even if it was impossible. I used three incidents to illustrate this for the reader. First, I chose the moment when he appeared in the director's office at the American Museum of Natural History, fresh out of school, begging for a job. When told there was no position open, Andrews insisted he didn't want a position—he just wanted a job. Surely they had to have someone to clean the floors. Why not him? The director couldn't believe that a youth fresh out of college wanted to clean floors, and Andrews agreed that he didn't want to clean just *any* floors. But the museum floors were special, and he'd clean them and love it if the director would just give him a chance. Andrews got the job and soon earned his chance to work on exhibit preparation as well as clean museum floors.

For the second incident I chose his excursion to recover the skeleton of a beached whale. He and his team worked frantically to dig the sinking bones out of the sandy beach and finally brought the complete skeleton back to the museum, where they were greeted with shocked admiration. A whale skeleton sank so quickly into the sand that a complete skeleton had never been salvaged. Everyone thought it was impossible. But no one had told Andrews that, and he pulled off the impossible feat.

The third anecdote you choose should be one of your subject's major accomplishments. For Andrews, I chose the risky expedition he led into the unexplored Gobi Desert in search of fossils that would help scientists understand dinosaurs and other prehistoric creatures more fully. What Andrews and his team discovered was the first evidence of how dinosaurs were born: They found the very first dinosaur eggs, some with the small skeletons of baby dinosaurs intact within them. In a time when the Gobi Desert was thought to be a wasteland beaten by sandstorms, Roy Chapman Andrews saw the possibilities hidden in the wasteland and made up his mind to go out and get them—and succeeded.

Kids love dinosaurs, so they're interested in reading about Andrews from the start. But you have to remember you're introducing a person to your readers—someone they'll want to make friends with and possibly emulate. So focus on what you want your readers to take away from meeting your subject, and choose moments in his or her life that show this in an exciting and inspirational way.

Read the Pros

1. Read *To the Young Scientist* by Alfred B. Bortz. See how the author focuses his interviews with famous scientists on the theme of nurturing an interest in science into a career.

2. Read special-interest magazines that profile adults in their fields. *Children's Digest*, for example, contains profiles of people in health and fitness professions who work with kids. *Boys' Life* features profiles of sports heroes, and people who have made contributions in the fields of science and technology.

3. Read *Sports Illustrated for Kids* magazine. See how the writers profile the careers of successful athletes.

TRY IT YOURSELF: REAL-LIFE ROLE MODELS

1. Practice interviewing a friend who's done something interesting—a neighbor who sells crafts, a friend who's started a home business or perhaps a fellow writer. Be sure to get your friend's complete professional name and correct spelling, title and business contact information (address, phone number, E-mail and fax), just the way you would when you wrote a profile. Make a list of questions to help you focus the interview, starting with:

   ★ What's the last project you worked on? Tell me about it.

   ★ What do you love about your work?

   ★ Is this what you wanted to do when you were a kid, or did you want to do something else? What? When did you start? How did you get into it?

   ★ Was there someone who encouraged you early on?

   ★ How hard is your job to do? What challenges do you run into?

   ★ Have you ever thought of giving up? What made you stick with this job?

   ★ What new projects do you have in the works?

2. Make a list of interesting careers that might appeal to young people. Keep this list in mind as you meet local celebrities or have an opportunity to meet celebrities from farther afield, and see if you can arrange an appointment.

An expert opinion from an expert

Interviewing an expert adds a human dimension to your nonfiction writing. If you want to write about the way string theory explains the fundamentals of matter to physicists, the topic can become awfully dry unless you put a face on it. If you can interview plain-spoken Columbia professor Brian Greene (who could multiply thirty-digit numbers by the time he was five), you can show kids his love for physics and math, and excite them about looking at the atomic chain—a subject they thought would be boring.

It's one thing to interview a neighbor who's done something exciting or even a celebrity who's appearing in the area, but how do you find an expert to interview? If you're writing about a field you're familiar with— suppose you're writing an article about writing for kids, for instance— you may have professional friends you can turn to. If it's a topic you studied in college, perhaps one of your old professors would be a good expert to interview or could recommend someone who would be even better. If all your research has been from print and Internet sources, however, you may not be able to rely on a personal referral.

Your library's reference section is a good place to start. Books like *Who's Who, Almanac of Famous People, Current Biography Yearbook, Facts on File World News Digest, Newsmakers,* and *Dial-an-Expert: The National Directory of Quotable Experts* can give you names and contact information for many professionals in different fields. Sometimes the print research you've done suggests that one specific expert might be the best one to contact for your article. That doesn't guarantee she'll be available and willing to do the interview, however. If the expert you're hoping to interview says no, ask if she can recommend another person in the field who might be interested. You're asking someone to take time out from her own work to help you do yours, so you need to be flexible and take what you can get.

If you have no idea how to contact the expert you want to interview, the Internet can help connect you. If you wanted to find Brian Greene at Columbia, you could start by exploring the Internet White Pages. Some people have unlisted numbers, however. In that case, go through the company or educational institution with which your subject is affiliated. Greene teaches at Columbia, so look for Columbia University, either by calling information, doing a general search online or by checking the list of American universities (http://www.clas.ufl.edu/CLAS /american-universities.html) and finding a link to Columbia there. From the university's home page you can go to their faculty listings by department. Look for Greene in the physics department, and you'll find contact information. Most faculty members have their office phone numbers and E-mail addresses shown, as well as a postal address. You can call or E-mail to request an interview. And if all you know is that Columbia University is doing important research in the string theory of physics, you could follow the links to the physics department and check out the courses offered. If the description of one of them includes string theory, see who's teaching it and follow up with an E-mail to that professor.

If your academic expert teaches at Cambridge in England, instead of the United States, the Internet can still find him. Check the list of international universities (http://www.mit.edu:8001/people/cdemello /univ.html) and follow the link to Cambridge. If you need an expert who works with a particular museum, perhaps a paleontologist affiliated with the Denver Museum of Natural History, you can go to a list of museums (http://www.icom.org/vlmp/) and use the link to go to the Denver Museum.

Explore the staff by department or send a query briefly explaining your project and asking how to contact the paleontologist directly.

Now you need to make the same personal connection you would make with an individual you wanted to profile. While the expert's field of expertise is the real subject of your article, as opposed to the expert himself, you still want to capture a sense of the scientist or researcher's personality. When your readers feels they know the expert personally, they'll feel they know the material better.

Conducting the interview

If you can meet with your expert and conduct the interview in person, you'll have the best opportunity to observe your subject in his work environment so you can show his mannerisms and personality, and even his surroundings, on the page—remember how much action can reveal about someone's personality. But a face-to-face interview isn't always possible. For your article about string physics, you may not be able to travel to New York to meet Brian Greene in person. That doesn't mean you should give up the idea of interviewing him. You could conduct the interview over the telephone, by letter, by E-mail, in a private chat room online, or by instant message if your Internet connection offers both of you that option.

Telephone interviews often work best, because both you and your subject will feel more relaxed and forthcoming talking to a live person. Writing letters and waiting for answers can be slow and formal in tone. E-mail or online chat interviews are more immediate, but people tend to write more cautiously than they speak, and their replies may sound stilted. When you speak on the telephone, you can hear the cadence and tone of your subject's voice, also. In writing you have nothing more than the printed words to go on.

Schedule the phone interview just the way you'd make an appointment to meet in person. Plan on thirty to forty-five minutes, but be flexible. If the interview is going well and your subject isn't in any hurry to rush off, you may be able to go up to an hour or longer. It's a good idea to take notes as well as tape-record the conversation. The notes serve as a backup in case your tape doesn't pick up every word perfectly, and they help you show the person more fully. Even if you can't see your subject, you can listen to the cadence of his voice, and note when he laughed or sighed. Use this as your write the interview. You can write:

> Greene chuckles. "Many of us in string theory see ourselves in the midst of a revolution," he says, his voice speeding up in his excitement.

This makes him come more alive for your reader than just writing:

> Greene believes that scientists in string theory see themselves revolutionizing the way people see space and time.

The combination of quote and description, even of only the way he sounds over a telephone, will capture your reader's interest more than the flat statement. When writing up a phone interview, use adverbs judiciously to modify tag lines—something you try to avoid overdoing when writing fiction. You can write:

> He said thoughtfully.
> She admitted ruefully.

Tags like these will help your readers feel they know the expert, and kids are more interested in listening to someone they've made friends with than to a distant stranger.

Taking notes serves another purpose, as well. Often you'll still be scribbling madly after the interviewee has stopped speaking. People feel very uncomfortable about silence and, while you're writing, your subject may say something to fill in the silence. These spontaneous comments that pop out often give you greater insight than some of the more carefully thought-out answers you'll get to your questions.

Especially if you live in a different time zone than your expert (it could be difficult to find a good time to telephone an archaeologist on site in Egypt, for example), E-mail can be the most convenient way to conduct the interview. Unfortunately, having to write a set number of questions in advance sacrifices the opportunity to pick up on something the expert says that might be unexpected. You can change direction when you're speaking face-to-face or over the phone, following the subject's lead, but if you handle it all in writing you don't have that luxury, unless you followup with repeat E-mails, which may irritate the interviewee after a while.

An Internet chat room or instant message system solves the problem by allowing you to communicate live. However, time is still a problem— the expert may have only so much time to spare for the interview, and people type more slowly than they can talk. But if you can't communicate in person or by phone, this may be your best solution. And one additional benefit is the fact that the answers are in writing, so there can be no question about the accuracy of your quotes.

After assimilating your expert's comments into the informational

TRY IT YOURSELF: INTERVIEWING

1. Practice interviewing a friend by E-mail. Explain what you're doing, and send the friend a list of questions that you think would give you enough information to explain a subject your friend is familiar with. If the information you get in the return E-mail isn't complete, plan out more detailed questions that might have gotten you all the information you needed. Keep this in mind when you conduct an E-mail interview with an expert for a manuscript you plan to sell.

2. Next time you chat with a friend over the telephone, make notes about the cadence of your friend's voice, when she laughs, shuffles papers or takes other actions during the conversation. Write a description of your friend based only on what you could hear while the two of you were on the phone. Keep this technique in mind when you interview an expert.

3. Select a topic you've been interested in writing about. Do an online or a library search to find an expert who could answer your questions about it. Complete your research for this article by telephoning the expert and arranging an interview. Pay attention to the vocal intonations, laughter, sighs and other reactions from your expert, as well as the quotes. Use these to fully describe the individual when you write the article.

portion of your article, run the final manuscript by the expert, even if the interview has been conducted in writing. Not only do you want to to insure that you've quoted him correctly, you also want to be certain that you haven't made a fundamental error in understanding either his comments or some aspect of the topic itself. E-mail can be extremely useful here, as it allows the subject to quickly read the manuscript, and copy it into his reply to make correction notes directly in the body of the text. If your subject isn't online, you can also fax the manuscript, and then follow up by phone to get any corrections.

Read the Pros

1. Read several issues of *Highlights for Children* magazine, paying attention to their nonfiction. See how the authors extensively quote field experts to support the narrative information in the articles.

2. Read *SuperScience* magazine. See how the writers often profile leading scientists and rely on their expertise to explain theories and support facts in informational articles.

3. Read several issues of *Muse* magazine. Here the writers quote scientists, historians, professors and naturalists to help young readers understand complex topics like electromagnetism or shooting stars.

VOICES FROM THE PAST
Kid-Friendly Biographies

Writing about someone you can interview has an advantage in that you can ask questions and get answers. One potential disadvantage is that the subject can disagree with your conclusions or ask you to change something you've written. When you write historical biographies, you're writing about people who have died, so they can't complain about what you write. It's more of a challenge to get to know a subject from history, however, because you're dependent solely on sources about the person. But you can get to know someone who lived in the fifteenth century or the fourth century B.C. remarkably well through research. It helps to start with a personal interest in your subject or the time in which he lived. The more personal you can make your biography, the more involved your readers will become.

Your goal is to know both who the person is and what the person does. People who become famous are well known for their achievements, so if you were writing about Thomas Edison, you'd want to fire the reader's enthusiasm for electricity as well as his interest in Edison as a boy and man. Just the way you familiarize yourself with the basics of a subject before you interview an expert in that field, you'll have to research the nature of your subject's work and understand it so you can explain it to the reader. To write a biography of Johann Sebastian Bach, you must understand his unique contribution to baroque music. Your biography of Bach will bring the composer to life by letting young readers share the thrill you experience at hearing his music.

Where to meet your subject

Since you can't string a telephone line a few centuries into the past to call your subject and chat, you need to find other ways to reach across time and meet this person. When I was researching English ruler Richard III, I started with published biographies and general books about the fifteenth century. These sources introduced me to my subject, but they also started me on a more detailed path of research.

As you read your preliminary sources, pay particular attention to the bibliography and footnotes. These will point you toward the sources that author relied upon, and if you check those sources you may find additional information that the later author found uninteresting or didn't have room for. Often these tidbits are just the sort of details that kids will love. One book about fifteenth-century history merely said that Richard was a loyal supporter of his brother, Edward IV, in Edward's battle for the throne. As I followed up sources, I found that Richard wasn't just a cheerleader, but a seasoned general who Edward trusted to lead his troops when Richard was still a teenager! Young readers would be impressed with that. The footnotes and bibliographies in these sources will, in turn, point you toward yet more sources.

Work your way back in time through these footnotes and bibliographies until you reach contemporary sources. You may be able to find biographies written about your subject while he was still alive, when the biographer may even have had a chance to interview him and some of the people who knew him. For people who lived in the past few centuries, these sources will include newspapers and magazines as well as books. Large public libraries and university libraries have collections of bound periodicals that go back to the early 1900s; other libraries may have them on microfiche or computer. Some newspapers and magazines from the 1700s and 1800s have been preserved in archives and museums, and bibliographies often cite the location of collections where you could view these. Newspaper articles from important periods, such as the Civil War or the Depression, may be reprinted in books, so you may be able to read a modern book that reprints older source materials without having to travel to archival sites to read the original.

Your subject is a real person and, like the characters you create, this person must be believable and complex on the page. Use all of these resources to discover as much specific and intriguing information as you

TRY IT YOURSELF: HISTORICAL SUBJECTS

1. Choose a historical figure who interests you. Go to the library and find some biographies about this person. Make a list of the sources you find in the footnotes and bibliography, including periodicals. See which of these you can find, and make a list of the different sources that the others cite. This list will work like map directions to lead you to your subject's personality.

2. Go to your library and select a bound volume of one newspaper or weekly newsmagazine for a particular year. Choose a famous person who made news that year. Go through the volume and make notes about each article you read about this person. How does the individual's personality evolve over the year, as you learn more about him or her? Do facts come out by December that were unknown in January?

---

can about your subject's life, accomplishments and personality. Young readers will be fascinated to meet this person whose achievements had an impact on so many lives.

Read the Pros

1. Read *Alexander Graham Bell: An Inventive Life* by Elizabeth MacLeod. See how the author includes reproductions of newspaper articles, manuscript pages and Bell's original diagrams to help readers get to know one of the major inventors of the telephone.

2. Read *And Then What Happened, Paul Revere?* by Jean Fritz. Here the author evokes the time of the American Revolution for the reader as well as letting the reader get to know Paul Revere. See how Fritz shares quirky facts about Revere, such as his whittling false teeth to earn extra money and his forgetting his spurs on the night of his dramatic ride to Lexington.

The personal touch—fact or fantasy?

If you're writing about someone who lived a long time ago, like Richard III, you won't find any handy newspapers or periodicals to refer to. That doesn't mean you won't be able to read contemporary sources, however. If you're writing about a commander under Caesar, you could refer to dispatches from the army that were sent back to Rome. You could also read Caesar's own writings about the Gallic Wars and the speeches of Roman statesmen in the Forum. You don't have to understand Latin to read these, either. Since this was an important period of history, scholars have collected these sources, translated them and published them. You'll be able to find published archival documents like these in university libraries or through interlibrary loan.

But contemporary documents of this type, while rich in period detail, may not be your most accurate source. People writing about their own times have a tendency to take sides and praise the side they agree with, while criticizing the opposite side. They don't yet have the perspective on the events that time will offer, so be sure that what you learn in a contemporary history fits with the rest of the information you're gathering about your subject.

Richard III lived in the fifteenth century, and a little research showed me that the Church kept track of news and history through the chronicles that monks wrote about recent events. Other members of the clergy and government wrote histories as well; for example, Sir Thomas More, who was actually alive while Richard was, wrote a history of his life and reign. I thought that the monks' chronicles and More's history would be excellent sources—until I started reading them. More describes Richard as a hunchback with a withered arm, born with a mouth full of teeth and a head of long, black hair. These were juicy details, but they didn't fit with the image of a teenage general leading his troops into battle. The picture of Richard hobbling along, clutching his battle axe (cited in numerous sources as his preferred weapon) in his one good arm while his other hung useless beside him, just wasn't convincing.

A little more research showed that, while More was indeed alive while Richard was alive, it was for a very short period of time. More was only a baby when Richard died. More was writing to please the Tudor ruling family who had taken the crown from Richard, and it was politically correct for More to denigrate Richard to show that the Tudors had the moral right to oust him and claim the throne. If I wanted to get to know Richard, I was going to have to dig deeper to find the truth.

Contemporary bias

Footnotes and bibliographies may also point you to private papers, letters, diaries and memoirs. Genealogical societies can be very useful in verifying family links, and you can often locate personal letters and papers in state historical societies or university collections. These can be wonderful resources because they give you a personal view of your subject and his times. However, remember that personal is not the same as factual. If a letter is written by a friend of Richard's, it will probably present him in positive light. If a diary is written by his enemy, it will probably contain only critical mention of him. But if an enemy wrote something positive about Richard, even if it was in a grudging tone, I would tend to believe it, because a critic wouldn't have any reason to exaggerate a good point. Likewise, if a friend or follower wrote something critical of Richard, it was probably an accurate assessment.

So how do you know who's telling the truth? Often historical research for a biography is like solving a mystery. You have to pay attention to what seems logical. If five sources say that Richard was born with a mouth full of teeth, but each source references Sir Thomas More's history, then that doesn't make the fact five times truer—it just means that the writers all trusted More's history as being truthful. If other evidence suggests that it isn't, you need to choose which evidence to discount and which to believe based on reason and your instincts about the subject's character.

Since you cannot question your subject, you may find it helpful to question one of his biographers. While I was researching Richard III, I made an appointment to meet with the British history professor who had most recently published a biography of Richard. I had some questions about his use of monks' chronicles, and he was happy to answer them and to discuss his research with me. His answers helped me evaluate the reliability of the chronicles and also the professor's opinion of Richard's character.

As you do more and more hands-on research and get closer to contemporary sources, you'll find yourself forming your own opinion of your subject's personality. That is the view which will eventually shape the tone of your biography and the character of this particular historical figure.

On location

One way to get to know your subject better is to travel to his home, if at all possible, and actually touch his things. Use your writer's imagination to transport you into his time, and look around. Examining furniture, clothes, tools, stonework and woodwork will show you a great deal about an individual—imagine how much your home might reveal about you to someone exploring it! I wandered through Richard's Yorkshire home and pondered the personality of a nobleman who chose to live where Richard did. I walked through his battlefields—both those where he won decisively and those where he was defeated. One of the most useful things I did was to study his library.

TRY IT YOURSELF: HISTORICAL PLACES

1. Compare a biography of someone you're already familiar with and that person's autobiography, diary or letters. What differences do you see between them? What conclusions can you draw about the person based on these differences?

2. Select a famous person from your region that you're already familiar with (perhaps a local author or a former politician). Do some preliminary research, then observe their home or grounds if they have been preserved. Make notes about what you see and what ideas these observations give you about your subject's personality.

3. Make friends with a local or regional museum worker. Explain your interest in writing biographies for kids, and get permission to handle some items in the museum collection that come from the same time period as your subject lived. If your subject was old enough to cook breakfast while World War I was being fought, examine a 1910 electric toaster and see how it worked. To practice describing your subject's daily activities, write a paragraph describing making toast for breakfast with this toaster.

Richard ruled England from 1483 to 1485. Caxton's first printed book appeared in 1477, so Richard's library wasn't extensive. Like most noblemen, he possessed only a few hand-copied volumes. But they were interesting. In addition to his wife's prayer book, which he had kept after her death, he had an English translation of Vegetius's *De Re Militari*, a book of military strategy. This was not common reading, even among noblemen who might be called to go into battle. It confirmed in my mind that Richard was first and foremost a general—being a statesman came only a distant second.

Walking where Richard walked, holding his actual books in my hands (the original copies are in the British Library, where any researcher may request them, and sit and read them) made Richard more real for me. It also allowed me to describe these locations and items accurately so that the reader felt he could see them for himself. If you're able to travel on location and do hands-on research, as well as read your subject's own words and the writings of his friends and enemies, you'll feel better equipped to sift through the multitude of facts and focus your subject's personality more sharply for your reader.

1. Read *Behind Rebel Lines: The Incredible Story of Emma Edmonds, Civil War Spy* by Seymour Reit. Edmonds was a Canadian woman who disguised herself as a man to spy on the Confederates for the Yankee Army. See how the author draws on U.S. Army records and files from the National Archives to help the reader get to know Edmonds.

2. Read *Behind the Mask: The Life of Queen Elizabeth I* by Jane Resh Thomas. See how the author includes a detailed bibliography and source notes for each chapter, showing writers how to dig for personal information on this Renaissance queen of England.

3. Read *Buffalo Gals: Women of the Old West* by Brandon Marie Miller. Here the author quotes memoirs and journals to introduce readers to women who lived in the Wild West of the nineteenth century.

Famous childhoods

Just as you should include at least one formative incident from your subject's youth or childhood when you write a profile, use childhood incidents to help the reader identify with the subject of your biography, before you go in-depth on the subject's adult achievements. One way to do this is to open with an exciting scene from childhood that shows the seeds of what will become a defining character trait or an early interest that will blossom into the subject's main achievements. For example, a biography of Wolfgang Amadeus Mozart might start with a scene in which the boy dazzles the court by playing one of his own compositions.

The catch is that you can have trouble finding out about your subject's childhood. When someone is a child, the people around him or her may have no idea that the youngster will grow up to be famous. These adults might not have taken note of the youngster or left any records. There's also the danger that later biographers may have made up incidents to demonstrate that their subject's unique qualities were evident in childhood, such as the apocryphal story of George Washington chopping down the cherry tree.

Sometimes children keep diaries, but not all of these survive. Childhood journals are often lost along with other childhood toys and school exercises. Keeping in mind the personality of the adult, pay attention to references that will allow you to glimpse childhood moments. Occasionally a famous person will write his or her own autobiography or a memoir.

TRY IT YOURSELF: FAMOUS CHILDHOODS

1. Read up on a figure from history who interests you. Find a childhood incident that reflects his later personality or achievements. Write this incident as an introduction to a biography of this individual.

2. Talk to some noteworthy friend about his or her childhood. Select some incident that you feel reflects the career the adult chose. Write up the incident using the dialogue and action your friend remembers.

3. Find out about a myth or tall tale involving a historical character you're interested in, such as Davey Crockett or John Henry. Do some research to contrast truth and myth. Write a few paragraphs showing what really happened and how the myth was born.

I drew on Roy Chapman Andrews's autobiography to write about him. An autobiography will tell you what your subject remembers of his own childhood and can give you some valuable material to work with. While you'll be taking it on faith that the subject's memory is accurate, his feelings about the memory will ring true, and these will help you and your reader feel closer to him on a personal level.

If you can't find enough material on your subject's childhood, kids will also relate to incidents in which the subject deals with children—either his own or anecdotes that involve other children. Kids may only be vaguely interested that Elisha Gray was one of the inventors of the telephone. However, they'll love the fact that Gray owed his discovery to his small nephew. When the boy was playing with his uncle's apparatus, he accidentally demonstrated how sounds of different pitches could be conducted through an electric wire. Gray went on to use this to patent this harmonic telegraph, the first step in the invention of the telephone, ahead of Alexander Graham Bell.

 Read the Pros

1. Read *Beryl Markham: Never Turn Back* by Catherine Gourley. The author focuses on Markham's childhood growing up in Africa. See how Markham's childhood experiences shaped her risk-taking spirit.

2. Read *Bach's Big Adventure* by Sallie Ketcham, based on a story Bach himself liked to tell about his boyhood. Through humor, the author shows how the

confident young Bach discovers that there is a greater organist than himself.

3. Read *George Washington: A Picture Book Biography* by James Cross Giblin. See how the author starts with Washington's childhood to establish his subject's love of family and home. In additional material at the end of the book, Giblin also examines the cherry tree myth.

Dramatic but accurate

Just the cut-and-dried facts about a person aren't enough to intrigue a young reader. It will help give your biography momentum if you use tension to carry the reader through your subject's life. This tension isn't something you'll just make up. A person who accomplishes noteworthy things has to work for them and often runs up against setbacks that make these goals difficult to achieve. As you plan out your biography, make the most of this tension to organize it, much the way you'd organize a fictional story with an escalating plot. In short, use fiction techniques to bring nonfiction characters to life. After all, while a biography may cover familiar territory for adult readers, most young readers will know only the barest outline, if that, of your subject's life. You can afford to develop the story with the unfolding tension of a novel.

Have a clear picture of the character in your mind, and start in the middle of the action to hook the reader, rather than merely starting by writing:

> Richard III was born on October 2, 1452. Before he was twenty, his world was in turmoil. Richard's brother, Edward, had made a dangerous bid for the throne. Risking his own security, the teenage Richard threw his lot in with Edward on the battlefield.

It's much more exciting for the reader to read:

> Richard peered into the fog. He could barely see the ranks of soldiers behind him and had no idea where the enemy line lay ahead. But the teenager knew his brother was depending on him. He signaled his standard bearer, and his banner, the white boar, flourished overhead.
>
> The boy stepped forward, his mouth dry. Would the men, most of them nearly twice his age, follow him? Could he possibly defeat the enemy army that faced him?
>
> Richard heard the steady shuffling of boots in the damp grass behind him. Despite his youth, the men were following.

203

"The white boar!" he shouted, and heard the cry echoed by the veterans at his back. He quickened his pace and his army charged.

An active opening like that will capture young readers' interest, and make them eager to find out more about Richard and how he found himself on the battlefield at the head of one wing of the army while he was still a teenager.

After crafting a dramatic opening, structure your development to show the struggles the subject had making his discovery or achieving her goal. A biography for beginning readers might end at the moment of achievement—a triumphant ending much like the climax and resolution of a fictional story. For older readers, however, you'll probably end with your subject's death. Given the dates in the past, the reader will be aware that the subject had died, so it won't be a depressing ending, especially if you show how this person's inventions or achievements live on.

Once you've planned out the organization of your biography, work to show your subject. If your subject lived this century and you're able to watch news films, you'll be able to describe appearance and mannerisms firsthand. Otherwise, pay attention to the way other authors describe the subject's actions, appearance and speech. Look at photographs of your subject. If possible, tape some of these photographs around your work area so you can keep the subject vivid in your mind as you write.

Speech is as important as appearance, possibly more. Remember that kids like to read dialogue. It will make the scene more exciting for your reader and will also show the subject more clearly in what he or she says. However, you can't just make up this dialogue unless you're writing historical fiction. In a biography you're limited to what you know your subject actually said. Since few people have been considerate enough to tape-record their conversations for posterity, you have to look to other sources to try to reconstruct dialogue.

Sometimes a diary entry or a letter to a close friend will report a conversation in detail. Sometimes the highlights of an important conversation will be written down as reference notes by one of the speakers, and you'll find these in your archival research. Occasionally a conversation will be a matter of public record, particularly in the case of official statements. Public debates may be printed in newspapers, and political arguments can be recorded in the Congressional Record. And someone who writes a memoir or an autobiography will often relate conversations

TRY IT YOURSELF: DRAMATIZING HISTORY

1. Choose a historical figure you'd like to write about. Decide what it is about this person that intrigues you—either the person's achievements or some quality that made those achievements possible. Write that at the top of a page in your character journal. Divide your page into three columns. In the left-hand column, make a list of things your subject set out to do. In the middle column, make a list of obstacles that made it more difficult for your subject to accomplish these things. In the right-hand column, make a list of ways the subject tried to overcome those obstacles. Use this organization to help you plan a biography of this person.

2. Based on your subject's achievements and struggles, choose one dramatic moment to open your biography. Plan how you would write this scene to introduce your readers to your subject.

3. Select a famous scene from your subject's life that many historians and biographers have portrayed. Make note of any dialogue reported in these sources. Write the scene, incorporating this conversation into it naturally so that the scene reads almost like a story, with action and dialogue.

---

as she remembered them. You'll be able to use the conversations in these sources to create dialogue in your biography. This dialogue will make the subject more believable, and the history you're writing more immediate for your readers.

Read the Pros

1. Read *Edith Wilson the Woman Who Ran the United States* by James Cross Giblin in the series Women of Our Time. See how the author brings Edith Wilson to life, both as a young girl and also as a woman, by using authentic dialogue taken from Wilson's autobiography and from the courtship letters that Edith and Woodrow wrote to each other.

2. Read *First Flight: The Story of Tom Tate and the Wright Brothers* by George Shea. See how the author interviewed Tom Tate's son in order to write about the boy who watched—and helped—the Wright Brothers succeed in their first flight at Kitty Hawk.

3. Read *The Road to Seneca Falls* by Gwenyth Swain. See how the author uses her

subject's speeches as well as her autobiography, diary and letters, in order to show how Elizabeth Cady Stanton made up her mind to prove that women could do something about their unfair position in society.

A little something extra

In addition to the facts of your subject's life and times, your subject will come more vividly to life for your reader if you include additional material. Because you're writing about a real person, paintings, sketches or photographs of that individual at various ages (childhood pictures are a must) will help the reader get to know the subject. Publishers often do their own photo research, but they won't always be able to find the pictures you feel are essential for your work. Sometimes the contract will be contingent on your ability to provide pictures or photographs. When I wrote about Maria Mitchell, I needed to supply photographs to clinch the sale. My research had already located the Maria Mitchell Association in Nantucket, and I found they were willing to supply photos for a modest fee. When I wrote about Roy Chapman Andrews, I was able to recommend that the art director contact the American Museum of Natural History for photos.

In addition to pictures, you can enhance readers' appreciation of your subject by helping them understand your subject's work. You might want to include a glossary of technical terms to invite readers into the subject's workplace. You can even share some of the excitement of your subject's activities, experiments or discoveries by including age-appropriate activities that the reader can carry out without parental supervision. For instance, a biography of Alexander Graham Bell might include an activity showing the reader how to build a string telephone.

To keep the subject clearly anchored in time, you might include a time line that integrates major events the reader would recognize with significant dates in the subject's life. You might even include sidebars that explain certain aspects of the historical period to help the reader become immersed in your subject's world.

Kid-friendly biographies invite young readers into a time machine that allows them to get to know fascinating people from the past. Fiction has a lasting impact on young readers because it allows kids to grow and change with the main character. Well-written biographies can have an even greater impact. In bringing historical figures to life for your readers, you're showing kids that real people, just like them, can grow up and accomplish amazing things that change the world. Long after your readers outgrow their childhood library, they'll remember their childhood heroes and be inspired by their achievements. And sometimes

TRY IT YOURSELF: A LITTLE SOMETHING EXTRA

1. As you research your subject, make a list of photographs of the person and the times, noting the source of each photograph (these will be shown beside the picture in print or on a copyright or photo source page). If you have access to a copier, make a photocopy of each picture and write the source on the copy. Keep these with your research notes to help you direct the art director to photos later on (or find them yourself if needed).

2. Make notes about an experiment or an activity your subject carried out. Decide how a reader could carry out a simplified version of it. Write a short how-to sidebar with directions for the reader to perform to see exactly what this person discovered.

3. Make a list of important dates in your subject's life. Do some research to add the dates of major historical events in the country where your subject lived and in the wider world. This time line will help you put your subject in the context of his historical period as you write the biography, and it will help your reader understand the subject and the time later on.

in writing historical fiction about real people, you can have the best of both worlds—as you'll see in the next chapter.

Read the Pros

1. Read *Lincoln: A Photobiography* by Russell Freedman. See how the author brings Lincoln vividly to life for the reader using period photographs and drawings as well as quotations from his writings and speeches.

2. Read *Charles Darwin: Naturalist* by Margaret J. Anderson. See how the author includes photographs to show Darwin in his times and how she gives readers activities and experiments they can try themselves to better understand Darwin's theories.

TRUTH IN FICTION

Fictional Characters From History

Sometimes you go so far into the world of a historical character that you can imagine this person beyond the limits of what historians record. You've moved into the realm of historical fiction. This can be a potent way to help young readers better see themselves in perspective as part of the human experience. Through reading historical fiction, kids discover that people share certain universal emotions and undergo similar experiences. And the fictional creation of vital characters with whom young readers can identify is the best way to help kids feel a personal stake in history.

When you write biography you are limited by the reality of what sources tell you. In historical fiction you are free to create a story in which fictional characters interact, believably, with historical characters. Your Revolutionary War story may be about Sarah who bakes Christmas cookies for George Washington's army at Valley Forge and speaks with the general herself. Or your adventure story about the age of exploration could feature Juan, a young page who accompanies Francisco Pizzaro's expedition to Peru and meets Atahualpa while the Inca ruler is Pizzaro's prisoner. The reader will still discover a great deal about Washington, Pizzaro and Atahualpa, but you can put words into their mouths that may not be recorded in any contemporary source. You can't rewrite history, but you can use your imagination to fill in the gaps that historical accounts inevitably leave.

In writing historical fiction, you plan a plot and develop characters who grow and change, just as you do in writing any fiction. But you ply your craft within the context of real history. That means you must do all the same research you would do if you were writing a biography in order to immerse yourself in the time period, and be sure that any facts you incorporate into your story about real people or events are accurate. However, instead of writing nothing but the facts, you create a fictional story that takes place around and during those historical events. This story should show modern readers how to grow and change in their time the way the historical character grew and changed in his. The first step is being true to the time period you're writing about.

True to the times

Kids feel the same desires and fears in any time period, but that desire will be expressed in different ways. Your research has shown you the historical events that occurred and the customs and costumes of the times. But your characters have to think like people who actually lived then. You can't put twenty-first century sensibilities into a twelfth-century character.

For example, you might choose to tell the story of a kid who wants to better herself and make a difference in the world. For a main character who lives today, you might choose Vilma, whose family came to America from Cuba. She wants to do extra well at middle school so she can get into a special high school for kids studying the sciences and go on to become a doctor. A character from the past might also want to better himself and make a difference—such as Cerdic, a young Saxon serf in twelfth-century England. However, Cerdic wouldn't entertain dreams of learning to read Latin so he could become a leech (an educated twelfth-century physician). This would give your readers an inaccurate impression of the period. It may be that most of the history that kids know comes from reading historical fiction, not from reading textbooks. The only exposure these young readers will have to twelfth-century Britain, third-century B.C. Rome or fourteenth-century Aztecs may be what they read in your novel, so it's your responsibility to be true to the times and people you write about. Perhaps Cerdic would try to learn herb lore from one of the older serfs and end up making a difference by helping treat wounded peasants in battle or healing serfs worn down by field labor.

If you want Cerdic to change so radically that he decides to shatter society's limitations and strive to free himself from his serf status, you'd have to introduce a dramatic or even explosive incident that would transform him beyond the expectations of his time, and make him seek something he never thought he could possibly have. Perhaps a neighbor warlord seizes the feudal estate that belonged to Cerdic's master and kills most of that previous lord's family. If the previous lord's young son escapes and Cerdic finds him but agrees not to tell, the young noble might repay Cerdic by teaching the serf to read while the noble hides out. If the son is rescued by his noble relatives, he might even take Cerdic and free him, and then Cerdic could dare to think he might get enough education to become a leech—but even that scenario would be pushing the envelope of believability.

To keep your historical fiction honest and accurate, immerse yourself completely in the period. Know domestic details involving clothing, food and household chores. Know what families did together in the evenings, how people traveled and how often they traveled, what tunes your characters might hum or sing, what you might see inside a character's cupboard or trunk or pocket—if clothing had pockets then! These are details you take for granted in writing about your own time. When you write historical fiction, however, you must research them until you think naturally like a character of the time you're writing about.

Resources writers don't always consider are books, stories and songs actually written during the period. If you're setting a story during the American Depression, go to a used bookstore or library and look for books, magazines and sheet music that were actually published during the early 1930s. Domestic details will be a natural part of this material. Your research will pay off—in a vivid evocation of the past that will draw your readers into the world of your story and allow them to get to know the characters in their true context.

 Read the Pros

1. Read *Johnny Tremain* by Esther Forbes. See how the author plunges the reader into the world of the American Revolution, showing John Hancock, Paul Revere, John and Samuel Adams and other figures of the period through Johnny's eyes. The unfolding of history, however, is just the background to Johnny's struggle to prove his identity and make a new life for himself after his hand is crippled.
2. Read *The King's Fifth* by Scott O'Dell. See how the author evokes the fifteenth-century world of conquistadors through young Esteban's account of his adventures. The history of the Spanish conquest of the New World provides the background for Esteban's murder trial.

TRY IT YOURSELF: TRUE TO THE TIMES

1. Select a historical period that you're familiar with from college research, a visit to a reconstructed historical site or family stories. Write about one day in the life of a youngster who lives then. Show how (and when) the youngster gets up, what clothes he or she puts on, what meals are served and what activities fill the day.

2. Imagine a modern youngster stepping through a magical mirror into a past time. Write what this youngster sees, hears and smells. How does this kid feel the past world compares to his or her own?

3. Imagine a youngster from a historical period you're familiar with who is magically transported into the present. Write the way this youngster interprets strange inventions like cars, computers, telephones or elevators.

---

3. Read *The Ramsay Scallop* by Frances Temple. Here the author shows Elenor and Thomas on pilgrimage, faithfully evoking the thirteenth century for the reader. The story shows how young people can find themselves on the cusp of change in a historical context, just as readers in the present feel the world is changing around them.

4. Read *The Shakespeare Stealer* by Gary Blackwood. When Widge is sent to steal the text of *Hamlet* for a rival theatre owner in Elizabethan England, he meets Shakespeare and other members of the company. Contrast this with *King of Shadows* by Susan Cooper, in which Nat Field finds himself transported back in time to join Shakespeare's company. See how Blackwood shows Shakespeare and the world of the Globe Theatre from Widge's believable sixteenth-century perspective, while Cooper shows the same world from Nat's twentieth-century perspective.

Transcend the facts to find the fiction

In writing a story or book about a historical character, keep fiction in mind as well as historical accuracy. You must plot a story in which a character who kids can relate to struggles to solve a problem in the context of historical events. To find your story problem, ask yourself what interested you about this historical character in the first place. What interested me about Richard III was the unsolved question of whether or not he had murdered his two young nephews in 1483 to get the crown. In essence, I was intrigued by a murder mystery. So I decided to write fiction instead of biography and solve the mystery.

To write *Tournament of Time*, I needed to find my way into a story that kids would be interested in reading. I suspected that young readers would care most about the young victims, two Princes who were approximately the readers' own ages It would be hard to write about them and about the mystery of their murder if they were still alive, so I decided to turn them into ghosts. For my main character, I decided to focus on a detective who would be faced with solving the Princes' murders. So I created Jessica, a modern girl whose family is haunted by the ghosts of the murdered boys. Jessica is also haunted by the spirit of their murderer, who is determined to keep her from finding out who really killed the Princes.

My research about Richard had shown me a great deal about his family and times. I used my imagination to go beyond that to examine Richard's nephews. What would it feel like to be a twelve-year-old boy who expected to be king and found himself displaced by his uncle and murdered instead? In developing the two murder suspects, Richard III and Henry Tudor (who took the crown in turn from Richard), I needed to create character and motivation. I used what I knew from my research about each as the basis for a character who might believably commit murder. Then I explored their lives—and their ghost lives—since the murder. How would it feel to have people suspect you of killing two children if you were innocent? After five hundred years, what would that character want—justice or revenge? To develop the murderer, I wondered what it would be like to keep hiding your crime for over five hundred years. That character would have to find ways of tangling truth, of blinding historians who looked as if they were about to solve the mystery. What would he do to a kid who was determined to expose him?

From the facts my research told me about the two Princes, I extrapolated to create kids with real desires, frustrations and resentments. From my research about Richard and Henry, I extrapolated to create powerful fifteenth-century rulers with believable hopes, fears, anger and determination. I couldn't have told the story that most interested me about Richard III and the mystery surrounding him if I had limited myself to dialogue that appeared in primary sources or facts that could be confirmed by other historians. None of the facts in *Tournament of Time* are inaccurate, but the story I crafted around them was fiction.

When your research leads you to ideas that go beyond documented facts, let those ideas lead you to historical fiction. Combine your writer's craft with the expertise you've garnered through your research, and plot a story that will inspire young readers to learn more about the period and the person who has captured your interest.

TRY IT YOURSELF: FIND THE FICTION

1. Choose a documented incident about a real person who interests you, such as Colonel Travis drawing the line in the sand at the Alamo. From your knowledge of the period, imagine what that scene might have been like. Write it from the central character's point of view, describing the setting and showing the character's thoughts and feelings as the scene unfolds.

2. Select a historical character you're familiar with. Imagine a situation in which the person found himself, but that isn't too well documented—for example, King Henry VIII talking to his son about becoming a king or Thomas Edison explaining to his teacher why he hadn't done his homework. Write the scene as you envision it, inventing dialogue and inner thoughts for the real person.

3. Now take the same historical character, and imagine a scene that wasn't mentioned in historical records at all, such as a family dinner or Christmas morning. Write the character's feelings about this fictional incident.

Read the Pros

1. Read *Dove and Sword: A Novel of Joan of Arc* by Nancy Garden. See how the author uses chronicles of the period and records from Joan's trial for heresy to show Joan through her young friend Gabrielle's eyes.

2. Read *My Dear Noel: The Story of a Letter From Beatrix Potter* by Jane Johnson. Based on the fact that *The Tale of Peter Rabbit* had its origins in a letter Potter wrote to a child in the Moore family, this picture book introduces young readers to the author-artist.

3. Read *Buffalo Bill and the Pony Express* by Eleanor Coerr. See how the author has used real events from Buffalo Bill's early life as a Pony Express rider to introduce beginning readers to the legendary historical figure.

Kids who view their times

If you choose a historical figure to be your main character, you'll have to do more than make up dialogue and inner thoughts as you write your story. Since young readers want to read about kids, focus on the individual's childhood, which may be undocumented. In this case you'll do all the other research to familiarize yourself with the person's life and times, but you'll have to go beyond that. Delve into his personality and come up with believable instances that might have occurred in childhood that would explain these traits.

For example, Richard was deeply loyal to his brother and acted in his brother's best interests, even if those were not Richard's own best interests. What might have happened in his childhood to generate such profound loyalty? I knew that Edward, the older brother, often visited his mother and his small brothers during his early struggles for the throne. Richard was slight and dark while the other children in the family were tall and fair—perhaps he was teased because he looked so different. Perhaps Edward took time out during those visits to be kind to the young Richard and praise the boy's talents, and Richard focused all his hero worship on the brother who would become king. I would be inventing this childhood bonding, but it fit with the facts, and it might just be true. In writing historical fiction, sometimes you have to follow your instincts.

Sometimes the historical personage you want to write about might be more interesting as an adult character than a child character. In this case, you could choose a peripheral figure to be the main character, either a real kid who lived during the time period or a fictional youngster you invent and place within the time period. For example, I might have shown the adult Richard from the perspective of one of his nieces. She would have loved her brothers and would be angry at their murder and determined to solve the mystery to know whether her uncle had killed them or whether the culprit was the young Tudor Prince who was making a play for the throne. In this case, I would have extrapolated from my research to transform this real girl into a well-rounded fictional character.

If a real character isn't near enough to the action, however, you may prefer to invent someone who might have been there but isn't mentioned. I could have invented a young page who was loyal to Richard—until the Princes were mysteriously murdered. He might suspect that his lord was guilty. As Henry Tudor's army approaches and the page knows that Richard will face Henry in battle, the boy must make up his mind about the murderer's identity so he will know whether he should follow his allegiance to Richard and stand fast beside him in battle, or run away to join Henry's army and fight against the noble lord he once followed.

This character might write a diary to tell his story. Several series for middle-grade readers feature a diary or journal format written by a fictional character or a fictional diary purported to have been written by a real youngster of the period. Sometimes your research will turn up actual diary entries that discuss the historical character you're writing

TRY IT YOURSELF: VIEW HISTORY AS A KID

1. Select a real historical figure who interests you. Based on what that individual eventually achieved or became, fabricate an incident in that person's childhood. Write a scene showing the incident from that person's perspective, using dialogue and action.

2. Choose a real historical person you're interested in. Create a young character who might come into contact with this person—a young piano student who has Beethoven for a teacher, for example, or an apprentice to printing press inventor William Caxton. Write a scene that shows what this youngster thinks about the historical character.

3. Choose a dramatic event from history that you're familiar with. Write a diary entry from the perspective of a youngster who's involved in it or witnesses it. For example, you might write about the signing of the Magna Carta from the point of view of a page serving King John. Or you might write about Commodore Perry landing in Japan from the perspective of a boy watching the foreigners stride across the mats that protected Japan's sacred soil.

---

about, and you can adapt these, or even use them as the basis for your story. Stepping outside of a famous historical figure can give you the perspective to show him more clearly. It can also give you the distance to craft an exciting story conflict that involves him, without requiring the real person to be at the center of a plot that was hatched solely in your imagination.

 Read the Pros

1. Read *The Bronze Bow* by Elizabeth George Speare. Here the author shows Jesus through the eyes of Daniel, a young Jewish rebel who starts out as a member of a group who want to force the Romans to leave Galilee, and is transformed by Jesus' teachings.

2. Read *Across the Wide and Lonesome Prairie* by Kristiana Gregory in the Dear America series. See how the author evokes the journey along the Oregon Trail through Hattie Campbell's diary. Look at other series that show readers what it's like to be a youngster participating in history being made. In *Elizabeth I: The Red Rose of the House of Tudor* by Kathryn Lasky in the Royal

Diaries series, the author shows the intrigues of the Tudor world through young Elizabeth's eyes.

3. Read *My Napoleon* by Catherine Brighton. The author has used Betsy Balcombe's journal accounts of Napoleon's time with her family during his exile in St. Helena as the basis for this picture book. See how the reader gets to know Napoleon through Betsy's eyes as the two become friends.

Kids who make history

Kids are most interested in reading fiction about other kids, so the most successful historical fiction often features real kids who found themselves making history. You may already know about a youngster who's done something generous or brave that has changed the course of history. That real boy or girl could make a strong main character in a story or book. If you're interested in a particular period of history, use your research to look for an event in which young people played a decisive role.

When I wrote *The Ghost Cadet*, I started by looking for an event in the War Between the States that involved kids. I found lots of incidents of brave little drummer boys, but I wanted to find kids playing a more decisive role. I found this in the Battle of New Market, fought in Virginia in 1864—a battle in which the youthful Corps of Cadets from the Virginia Military Institute changed the battle's outcome. As Confederate General Breckinridge marched to New Market to face a large Union force, he called out the Corps of Cadets to join his small army. Unwilling to risk the boys' lives (some were as young as fifteen), the general kept them back as a reserve. When Union cannon and musket fire shattered the thin Confederate front line, however, General Breckinridge had no choice but to order the Corps of Cadets to fight.

I began thinking about those boys and how they must have felt marching into battle for the first time. From my research I knew that the Confederacy's position was so precarious by 1864 that supporters who were actually too young or too old to fight were desperate to be accepted into the Army. I decided that the Cadets would be proud that the general had called them out. Not everyone agreed with the general's decision, however. From the survivors' accounts of the battle it was clear that the regular Army veterans were not pleased at all. As the boys marched past, the veterans would sing "Rock-a-Bye Baby," and they'd tease the Cadets, saying they should run home because their mothers were calling them. I decided this would have made the boys even more determined to prove themselves under fire.

My interpretation of their probable mood was supported by their actions in battle. When the reserve was committed, the Cadets formed ranks as if they were on Sunday dress parade. Several boys were hit and fell as they advanced under the heavy fire, but the Cadets closed ranks and marched on. They took their place on the front line and, when the advance was sounded, the boys double-timed it toward the Union position, quickly outstripping the veterans. They reached the firing line before the Union soldiers were able to pull off the cannon in retreat, and the Cadets captured the cannon. The boys' courage under fire inspired the veterans, and at the end of the day General Breckinridge told the Cadets that the Confederacy owed the day's victory to them—the battle could not have been won without them.

This was a real event in which real kids made a difference, and I knew this would be the basis for my book. From my research about Southern society, I felt that family loyalty and heritage were decisive in at least some of the boys' motivation, and that was what I decided to write about. I wanted to see whether the sacrifice was really worth it— and the only way to explore that was to write about one of the boys who had given the greatest sacrifice of all: his life. Of the 257 boys who fought, 47 were wounded and 10 died, so I decided to choose one of those 10.

When fiction works

Because I knew that readers would be more interested in reading about a young Cadet than an older boy, I narrowed the group down to several of the youngest. But I was also already thinking about the story. I needed a reason for the Cadet to become a ghost haunting the battlefield. Because I was interested in family heritage, the reason had to involve family. I finally decided that my Cadet had lost something of such value to his family that he couldn't rest until it was found, but I couldn't think what that might be. My husband comes from an old Virginia family, and I thought he might have a suggestion based on his personal sense of family heritage. He did. He suggested that the boy had lost a pocket watch that had been passed down to him by his father or grandfather.

I liked the idea and decided that my ghost Cadet had been wearing his family watch as he marched into battle. When he felt himself shot and realized he was about to die, he made up his mind to hide the watch where it would never be found by scavengers if the Union side won the battle—but he hid it so well that no one found it even though the Confederacy won. Until the watch could be recovered and returned to his family, he had to haunt the battlefield, searching for someone alive to help him. Once I had the central mystery of the plot worked out, I hid my fictional watch in a real place on the battlefield, where it might believably remain until the present. Then I looked to see which of my candidates had died nearest to this place. Only one of the younger Cadets had fallen in the vicinity: Cadet William Hugh McDowell.

Biographical information about him was sketchy, but I noticed that his middle name, Hugh, was his grandfather's first name. Perhaps his grandfather could be the one to give my fictional Cadet his watch. Perhaps his parents were disappointed in the boy for some reason, increasing his need to prove himself to his family. In plotting my story, I balanced the fictional ghost of Cadet McDowell with Benjy. A modern boy whose father has abandoned his family, Benjy had no sense of his own family heritage. As my fictional Cadet told Benjy about his family and the missing watch, he inspired Benjy to learn more about his family. At the same time, McDowell's personality and character began to take shape in my mind. His father didn't think he'd amount to much, and his mother spoiled him. The time he spent at VMI was his happiest time, because he made friends who accepted him.

When I was about halfway through writing *The Ghost Cadet*, I had an opportunity to visit VMI and do some additional research in their Archives. I read for the first time the letters that the real Cadet McDowell's family had written to the Institute about their son—letters from his mother, first enrolling "Willie" and then writing to say he'd be late arriving because he'd twisted his ankle. His father immediately wrote another letter saying that "William" would be along directly. This fit perfectly with the mama's boy I had imagined! But then I read two later letters in Cadet McDowell's correspondence folder that took me completely by surprise.

After the news that his son had been killed in battle, the elder McDowell wrote back to the commander, expressing his shock and giving instructions for the return of his son's personal possessions—including his son's watch. A subsequent letter expressed dismay that the watch could not be found. My research, combined with my imagination and my character craft, had resulted in a startling coincidence. The real Cadet McDowell had, in fact, actually owned a pocket watch that had been passed down through his family, just like the fictional watch that my husband had suggested and that I had used as the basis of my imagined mystery. The McDowell family watch has never been found since the Battle of New Market.

When you do careful research, then employ all of your character craft to immerse yourself fully in the world of a real person, you may imagine, and even discover, truths. You have to rely on a certain amount of intuitive instinct as you try to reconstruct history. That instinct is something a fiction writer can use that a pure scholar cannot. But that will make this character from the past come to life for you as you write his story—and for the youngster who reads it.

TRY IT YOURSELF: KIDS IN HISTORY

1. Choose a historical period that interests you. Find a general history text of the period at the library, and go through it, making notes about events that involved real youngsters. Pick one incident and plan a course of research that will help you get to know this youth and develop him as a fictionalized character in a story.

2. Take a youngster who participated in a historical event, such as the Cadets at New Market. Based on your knowledge about the incident and about characterization, make notes about what the youngster's motivation might have been, what she hoped to achieve and how she reacted to the way the event worked out.

3. Select a real youngster who achieved something in history, such as the young Mozart performing in court. Write about the event from the young character's perspective, sharing his thoughts and feelings with the reader.

 Read the Pros

1. Read *Keep the Lights Burning, Abbie* by Peter and Connie Roop. See how the authors write a fictionalized account of Abbie Burgess's courage based on her own accounts and other historical sources. When her father (the lighthouse keeper) is stranded during a severe 1856 storm, Abbie struggles to keep the lighthouse off the coast of Maine lit throughout four long weeks.

2. Read *The Courage of Sarah Noble* by Alice Dalgliesh, based on true accounts of Sarah Noble's venture into the Connecticut wilderness with her father in 1707. Here the author develops a believable character in eight-year-old Sarah as she survives in the new homestead, waiting for her father to return with the rest of their family.

3. Read *Kate Shelley and the Midnight Express* by Margaret K. Wetterer. See how the author turns the real fifteen-year-old Kate Shelley into a memorable character as Kate risks her life to prevent a passenger train from crossing a broken bridge.

EPILOGUE

In the midst of reading *The Proving Ground*, a young reader turned to his mother and asked, "How does she know what it's like to be a teenage boy?" When his mother told me the story, she explained that he was amazed that fourteen-year-old Kevin's thoughts and feelings were so like his own, yet had been written by an adult woman.

How did I do it?

Now that you've finished this book and created so many characters in the Try it Yourself Exercises, you know how I did it. And you can do it yourself with your own characters.

An editor once told me that a short story I'd sent in was too long, that the vocabulary was too advanced for the age group the story was best suited to and that the cast was too large—but everyone who had read the story loved the main character. They wanted to buy the manuscript and were sure I could fix those other minor problem areas.

Strong, colorful characters will move both readers and editors, and can be your passport to publication. So get out your character journal and start writing—kids out there are waiting impatiently to meet your characters.

INDEX

Printed in the United States
62530LVS00004B/80